Feeling Good About Yourself

A Guide for People Working with People Who Have Disabilities Or Low Self-Esteem

by
Gloria Blum, M.A. and Barry Blum, M.D.

**Self-Esteem ♦ Socialization Skills
Sex Information ♦ Decision Making
Assertiveness ♦ Preventing Victimization**

Feeling Good About Yourself

A Guide for People Working with People Who Have Disabilities
Or Low Self-Esteem

Self-Esteem
Social Skills
Sexual Information
Preventing Victimization
Assertiveness
Decision Making

by

Gloria Blum, M.A.   **Barry Blum, M.D.**

**Blue Tower Training Center
MACON RESOURCES, Inc.
P.O. Box 2760
Decatur, Illinois 62524
United States of America
www.maconresources.org**

****

This edition copyright © 2004 by Gloria Jeanne Itman Blum and Barry Blum. All rights reserved. Printed in the United States of America. No part of this publication may be reproduced, stored in a retrieval system, or transmitted, in any form or by any means, electronic, mechanical photocopying, recording, or otherwise, without the prior written permission of the publisher.

First Printing, Academic Therapy Publications, 1977
Second Printing, Feeling Good Associates, 1981
Third Printing, Feeling Good Associates, 1986
Fourth Printing, Blue Tower Training Center, 2004

ISBN: 1931568308

Library of Congress Control Number: 2004108542

HOW TO USE THIS GUIDE

The first half of this guide is devoted to the understanding and development of skills in the area of self-esteem, socialization awareness and interpersonal relationships. The second half focuses on specific areas of human sexuality and sex education.

The table of contents identifies broad topics covered in each section. The titles and headings within each section identify activities used to teach each topic. Learning objectives for those activities are included. For certain activities we have included appropriate maturity levels.

The italicized paragraphs are real-life stories illustrating or clarifying the subjects addressed. The items in the shaded boxes are "Building Blocks" for learning self-esteem and appropriate behavior, which deserve additional emphasis.

CONTENTS

Introduction to Self-Esteem, Socialization Skills and Sex Information 7

Principles of Self-Esteem 10

Techniques for Teaching Self-Esteem 11

Teaching People Who Are Slow Learners 24

Relating to Others - Social Behavior 28

The Yes-No Process: Preparation for Decision Making 32

To Whom Can You Go For Help? 50

Developing Socialization Skills 55

Relationships and Dating 56

Sex Roles 63

Feeling, Recognizing and Dealing With Emotions 67

Experiencing Oneself Through the Senses 74

Training Staff and Parents as Sex Educators 79

Preliminary Inventory of Personal, Social and Sexual Experiences and Attitudes 85

Getting to Know One's Body/Sexual Self-Awareness 86

Sexual Activity 92

STD (Sexually Transmitted Disease), Including AIDS 109

Homosexuality 114

Sexual Independence 118

Appendix A: Four Model Individual Educational Plans (IEPs): 121

Appendix B: Helping Parents Deal With the Sexuality of Their Son or Daughter with Special Needs, by Winifred Kempton, M.S.S. 126

Resources 129

PREFACE TO THE FOURTH EDITION

Since it's initial publication in 1977, *Feeling Good About Yourself* has continued to be used by educators, therapists, teachers and parents all over the world. With each new edition, sections of this book have been added, old sections brought up-to-date and outdated portions removed. Since the last edition the world has changed considerably as the Human Immunodeficiency Virus (HIV) has spread around the globe. The need for sex education, especially to prevent victimization of vulnerable people, has taken on a new urgency. This newest edition is still based on the assumption that the cornerstone of responsible sexual behavior and responsible sex education is self-esteem and that it must be role modeled and taught first, along with socialization skills, before a human sexuality program can be offered to any student population. We hope that this new edition will be as useful to you as the previous editions have been for our earlier readers.

Gloria & Barry Blum, Kailua-Kona, Hawaii, June 2004

ACKNOWLEDGMENTS

Special thanks to Dr. Sol Gordon for his wisdom and skill in reviewing this work in all its various stages.

Thanks also to Winifred Kempton, M.S.W., Stella Resnick, Ph.D., Betty Dodson, Ph.D. and Jean Edwards, Ph.D. for their advice and support.

Thanks to Joel E. Gimpel for his expertise in proofreading the manuscript and to Stephen Denzer, M.D. for his review of the medical information.

INTRODUCTION

I saw Gloria Blum in action before I ever read the first edition of her book, **Feeling Good About Yourself**. It's difficult for me to convey how excited I became when I witnessed a lethargic, unresponsive group of young mentally retarded adults come alive within a period of less than one hour. The exercises in this book work; the concepts are valid; and the results are the equivalent of miracles.

Now, some years later, after accumulating much evidence, I am equally impressed, and I can't think of a better definition of self-esteem than the one suggested in this book: that "self-esteem develops from the process of learning how to give oneself approval, as well as learning the process of behaving responsibly toward others." For a long time I have felt that the key dimension missing in the area of teaching people who are slow learner has been providing socialization skills which promote self-esteem and social responsibility.

At last we have a curriculum that is both inspiring and operational. I am deeply grateful to Gloria Blum and her husband/collaborator and I am proud to serve as an affirmation for their work. This fourth edition is a testimony to two people who are constantly exposed to and learning from new experiences.

Sol Gordon, Ph.D.
Author and Prof. Emeritus
Child and Family Studies
Syracuse University

INTRODUCTION TO SELF-ESTEEM, SOCIALIZATION SKILLS AND SEX INFORMATION

SELF-ESTEEM

Self-esteem involves a process of learning how to give yourself approval - that is, learning how to say to yourself, "I am OK." It may not come automatically. It's something that is learned. Self-esteem is not narrow self-interest, self-absorbed concern nor raising yourself up by putting others down, nor is it selfish so-called good intentions often bringing pain to others. True self-esteem is enriching to one's community and environment as well as to oneself.

It's first learned by relating to the people in your lives close to you who "appreciate their own worth and importance and have the character to be accountable for themselves and to act responsibly toward others." [California Legislative Task Force on Self-Esteem, 1990].

The pregnant mother who feels good about herself conveys this positive attitude toward her baby. On a simple physiologic level, such a mother is likely to take good care of herself. She will eat and exercise and rest appropriately and thus benefit her fetus as well as herself.

On a conscious level, many pregnant mothers report experiences of communication with their unborn offspring. "Whatever the fetus picks up, the relationship between mother and child is enhanced. The fetus knows no separation from its mother. When the mother feels anxious, the fetus feels anxious. When the mother feels content, the fetus feels content." [Leni Schwartz, *The World of the Unborn*, 1980, Marek, NY]

There is no significant correlation between self-esteem and I.Q. Findings indicate that intelligence is generally associated with feelings of personal worth; but one cannot assume that this condition (intelligence) is the major and overwhelming influence in the development of self-esteem. The findings indicate quite clearly that depression tends to be related to low self-esteem. One's self-esteem is not dependent on any one factor alone, such as academic achievement, but on a complex combination of factors.

Students who are slow learners or people with low I.Q. may not be able to read as well as more intellectually gifted persons. They may have more difficulty making change in a store. In fact, many supposedly "normal" people have difficulty making change. They just know how to cover it up better. People with disabilities can be just as intuitive or just as musical as anyone else; they can fall in love just as easily; they can laugh just as readily; they can be friends just as capably; but not if they are blocked in advance and then *conditioned* by stereotyped prejudices.

ORIGINS OF SELF-ESTEEM

After birth and bonding, we know no separation from our mother. Her face, her breasts, her love and smiles are part of our presence with no awareness of separateness. As we grow up, we learn to differentiate ourself from our environment. We begin to individuate and develop our own perspective and desires and will.

If a child is wanted and the future parents are prepared to become parents, the child will likely be lovingly cared for. This process will usually be natural and easy. If a pregnancy is unwanted or feared, if the infant is not loved, if the parents are not prepared, the oneness of bonding may be blocked.

The role models in our immediate environment (mother, father, siblings) give us our first lessons in self-esteem. If they approve of themselves and treat us and others and themselves with respect, we learn from them how to feel good about ourselves.

Dr. Peter Koestenbaum, a philosopher and writer, has said that it is during the first year or two of a child's life when the child develops the ego that will serve that individual throughout life. This comes directly from a mother's love. You can not spoil a child with too much love or attention during those first years!

When we approach age two, we learn to speak and express our individuality by using the powerful word "no!" that we learned from our parents. We call this period the "terrible twos" because we are clearly separating ourselves from our parents. We are setting limits to our parents' authority over us. Wise parents will honor their child's "no" if they want their sons or daughters to become confident, independent and interdependent adults who are not available for victimization and seek help when needed. As we grow up, we continue to individuate as we compete in school, make friends and incorporate aspects of those people's personae to our personalities, thus choosing how we will behave and appear in society.

As we get older we continue to individuate, seeking and creating identities that define us and separate us in our search for our self. We learn some skills and leave home to attend school or work where we compete and compare ourselves to our peers. During that competing and comparing we experience judgment, jealousy and perhaps failure. We often feel alone and left out of the flow of life.

As an individual, we may become aware of a craving for the giving and receiving of love and oneness. As we grow spiritually, we may begin to realize that the separation of trying to prove our individuality doesn't feel good any more… in fact, it's lonely and no longer fulfilling.

We then may choose to undo the patterns of individuation to come back to the oneness we crave which feels more genuine and comforting than separateness. We may choose to stop competing to try to prove ourselves worthy of others' approval. We may deliberately stop judging others and ourselves. We may take responsibility for uncomfortable feelings of separation such as jealousy and interpret it as a need to feel included and feel whole.

As we evolve back into the gift of oneness, the gift we were born into, we learn to accept or redesign our concept of parents and incorporate within ourselves a beneficent mother and father worthy of trust to nourish the child within. We begin to feel whole and part of something greater than our small self - a more inclusive Self that fearlessly includes others' welfare as part of our own well being.

Happy days and frustrating days, good times and bad, are parts of living. With an underlying steady sense of self-esteem and self-acceptance, the ups and downs become part of the process of living. Problems become situations needing solutions. Temporary thirsts and hungers become opportunities to appreciate nourishment even more. These challenges, when successfully overcome, serve to strengthen us and enhance our own sense of capability.

We learn about ourselves through our achievements and mistakes. Mistakes are lessons that teach us how to handle situations in a new way. When we experience a sense of success and completion in our daily lives - a sense of productiveness, usefulness and a sense that we are making a difference to others - we gain a good feeling about ourselves. Those good feelings are building blocks for gaining courage to take risks from which we grow and gain self confidence.

DON'T BE AFRAID TO FAIL
(Published in the Wall Street Journal © 1981 United Technologies)

You've failed many times,
although you may not remember.
You fell down the first time you tried to walk.
You almost drowned the first time you tried to swim,
didn't you?
Did you hit the ball the first time you swung a bat?
Heavy hitters, the ones who hit the most home runs,
also strike out a lot.
R.H. Macy failed seven times before his store in New York caught on.
English novelist John Creasey got 753 rejection slips before he published 564 books.
Babe Ruth struck out 1,330 times but he also hit 714 home runs.
Don't worry about failure.
Worry about the chances you miss when you don't even try.

SOCIALIZATION SKILLS

Self-esteem develops from the process of learning how to give yourself approval. Social learning develops from the process of gaining awareness of outside approval and disapproval and being accountable for yourself and acting responsibly toward others. Because we do live among others, our behavior is almost always subject to others' approval or disapproval. We learn socialization skills by constant practice. When we are fortunate enough to have effective role models around us, we learn what behaviors are appropriate to our environment. Since there are many different environments in our society, we also learn principles of behavior for teamwork in a variety of settings.

People who "look different" or "act different" (for instance, persons with disabilities) and/or who may be unaware of how they appear to others need to learn how to act "normal" (that is, how to behave appropriately in public). If they've been raised in a sheltered environment such as a hospital or institution, they may not have experience in "normal" everyday social interactions. Routine dress or behavior, even the usual conversation in a state hospital ward, is not what is common behavior outside. When the resident leaves the protected environment of the hospital, he or she will be exposed to the risks of victimization (and even in the hospital there are, unfortunately, situations wherein residents can be victimized). Shopping for clothing or buying meals or having the right change for the bus aren't skills normally acquired in the hospital or residential care facility or even in the overly protected home. How to relate to strangers is a social skill acquired by practice and experience. When these experiences have been limited or are altogether lacking because of the need for special care and protection during the growing years, such a person will still have to learn these skills in some way before he or she can live comfortably within the community at large.

SEX INFORMATION

Sexual feelings aren't learned. They arise in all human beings at one time or another. Sexual behavior is taught. Each society has its own set of rules of acceptable and appropriate behaviors. When sexual behavior is solitary, for instance masturbation, there are acceptable (and unacceptable) times and places for it. When sexual behavior involves another person there must be agreement or permission with that other person, besides whatever societal conditions might exist. Hugh Prather in "Notes to Myself" asks, "What is the difference between 'I want food' and 'I want sex'?" The answer is: "consent."

The how, where and what of sexual behavior is usually taught covertly to most of us. We get mixed messages, conflicting reports and a lot of misinformation. Hopefully, we sort it out eventually and since we usually don't share a lot of accurate information about sex with friends, we accept what information we have, and make do. Some of us are lucky and have generally satisfactory sexual lives. Some are not so lucky and have generally unsatisfactory sex lives.

Some of us, however, have some physical limitations to our mobility or emotional limits to our socialization experiences or intellectual limitations on how to deduce facts from the great supply of contradictory information on sex that is publicly available. These people are at a disadvantage until they do learn what is going on. They can be frightened by their own <u>normal</u> feelings; they can be victimized by other people's inappropriate behavior. Sex education provides the knowledge for appropriate choices.

Note: *One of the most effective ways that the material in this guide can be presented is by a man and a woman together. For many students this male-female model may be the only one they will experience in a personal and direct way. This is especially so for people living in an institutional environment. The man and woman presenting this program need not be related or married, and they need not agree on everything. Men and women (people, that is) often disagree. But working together and relating in an honest, open, human and mutually respectful manner, is a profoundly valuable model for any student or client.*

PRINCIPLES OF SELF-ESTEEM

With repeated experiences of success and completion as well as lessons learned from mistakes, we start experiencing a sense of our own inner strength and personal control over our own lives. Rather than feeling like victims, we see ourselves as the creative forces in our own lives. We learn how to say "yes" and "no" and really mean it. A part of learning how to say "yes" and "no" and meaning it with confidence is for people to actually listen to us and acknowledge and respect our decisions. Inner strength and personal power come from our experiences of successful assertive action as well as responsive acknowledgment from our environment. The ways we receive reinforcement for our assertiveness, independence, decision making and risk taking will greatly influence our experience of success and completion and confidence.

CREATING A SAFE SUPPORTIVE ENVIRONMENT

Because the feeling of belonging to a group or family is so valuable for the development of self-esteem, the first step in establishing this program is the creation of a safe and supportive environment. Establishing a one-to-one relationship between leader and participant before meeting as a group can be most effective. The student has an opportunity to feel special in relation to the leader. Voiced breathing, *Feeling Good Playful Question Cards,* Individual Strength Assessments with positive feedback and other success-oriented activities in this Guide all build positive feelings of trust.

> Provide a supportive environment where the participants feel safe. In such a setting they are exposed to an attitude of unconditional respect and love. Whatever the participant offers is accepted unconditionally with expressed appreciation. We intentionally applaud or reinforce every contribution by every participant in order to encourage a willingness to participate more freely.

INAPPROPRIATE BEHAVIOR

If someone's participation is not appropriate, then that's an opportunity for teaching. It is not a time to put anyone "on the spot." Instead, you may first simply repeat what the person said or describe their behavior objectively and then ask the group, "What happens when you do that? What are the consequences of that action? Is there another way of doing it or saying it?" If a suggested solution is not appropriate, brainstorm a more appropriate response and transform the problem into a learning situation.

MATURITY LEVELS

Maturity levels are shown for suggested activities. These are guidelines referring to the level of the group or class member's verbal abilities, self and social awareness and general level of understanding. Chronological age is not the primary determinant. Because their abilities and levels of awareness may be so varied, group participants will differ as to how they learn the concepts taught. Frequent and varied review of these activities is necessary to reinforce and reevaluate how well these concepts are learned and applied to real life situations.

TECHNIQUES FOR TEACHING SELF-ESTEEM

The following are specific objectives for learning:
1. To encourage a safe, supportive environment.
2. To create an environment of reliable acceptance.
3. To create an environment of unconditional appreciation.
4. To remove barriers to expression and communication.
5. To encourage independent participation and risk taking.
6. To develop and reinforce attitudes and techniques of caring and loving, rather than those of confrontation and competition.
7. To encourage positive self-image.
8. To encourage student/participant leadership roles and experiences.
9. To emphasize use of group dynamics techniques to keep the energy light, positive, and the pace moving.

BRAINSTORMING

We will refer to the technique called "brainstorming" frequently in this Guide. The leader asks the group for ideas or answers to questions. The leader or an alternative scribe writes ALL the answers given onto a board or pad for all to see. All ideas are accepted. No suggestions are criticized. Later, those ideas are reviewed and reconsidered. Sometime during that review the responses may be ranked in order of applicability or some responses may be tactfully discarded. The important point is that when the ideas are first offered, there is never criticism or rejection of any contribution.

PRINCIPLES
There are two self-esteem principles to keep in mind. The first is:

> Each of us is unique and individual <u>and</u> We are also like other people.

This principle applies to all of us with no exception. We all need to be recognized, respected and appreciated as worthy, unique individuals with our own unique mission and contribution to humankind, our own needs, feelings, strengths and abilities, preferences and our own lessons in life to learn.

We also need to be recognized, respected and appreciated for being like other people, an equal and an included member of the human race (i.e. society).

We all have and need a mission in life. That mission is to help and serve others and to help and serve ourself. Balance is essential in our mission. We give enough to enable others and ourself. If we give too much (for approval, money, love, etc.) we feel used, victimized or drained, like a martyr; we become ill and we resent others. On the other hand, when we are too self-absorbed we cease to serve others effectively and we fail in our mission to make a difference.

"If I am not for myself, who will be for me? If I am only for myself, what am I? If not now, when?" Rabbi Hillel, Ethics of the Fathers.

We need a balance between our sense of separateness and our sense of being like other people. When we are out of balance and feel and look too unique and different, we feel like we stick out like a sore thumb. We feel stared at and judged for being too different, too unlike others. We receive too much attention.

During a brainstorming session on how to handle these situations, one of my clients shared that when she was on the bus and someone stared at her, she smiled at them and said: "Gee, you stare good!" This client was a great teacher for me and had a unique sense of humor. What a happy way to break the ice. Everyone laughs and relaxes and feels like friends.

If on the other hand, if we feel we are too much like other people, then we feel invisible, unnecessary, faceless, an unnoticed part of a crowd, and we feel that we can be replaced. We all long to be recognized as a necessary, worthy part of a team.

A myth about productivity that you may have come across if you work in any large office or organization is that people perform better when they are reminded that they can be replaced. The attitude that goes with this is that "we can get along without you, so you better keep in line." That is a myth and it is destructive to self-esteem. The message you want to communicate is: **"We are not complete without you."**

Doesn't that feel better? People perform best when they feel this attitude around them. It inspires people to think new ideas, and to take risks, and to put more into their work. Every agency director should have a policy sign on his/her door that says: "WE ARE NOT COMPLETE WITHOUT YOU." Watch how productivity rises!

A way to implement this philosophy may occur when a member of your team or group arrives late. Instead of berating them, say to them and everyone else in the room, "Now we are complete." You may soon notice people arriving early because they feel needed.

Point out and acknowledge to people how taking personal risks can pay off in: authentic communication; listening to our intuition, our inner knowing; expressing creativity; really involving and evolving in our job with a sense of belonging and comfort.

> **Self-esteem is not exclusively the process of feeling unique and individual. Self-esteem includes a balance with a sense of belonging, a sense of inclusion that is rooted within a deeper knowing that each of us is also like other people.**

REINFORCEMENT TECHNIQUES FOR DEVELOPING SELF-ESTEEM

1. Making eye contact.
   The eyes are like the windows for the soul to shine out and connect to other souls. If the windows are not open, no one can enter or come out to connect and communicate. The result is a cold, uncomfortable, mechanical, unfulfilling waste of precious time for everyone. As a facilitator you have the opportunity to make a difference with others and yourself by simply dropping judgment and shining your radiant presence into another's eyes. The warmth and trust will become the foundation for learning and change and self-esteem.

   Some cultures consider eye contact disrespectful with authority figures but we have heard representatives from those cultures say "that has to change" because the abuse that accompanies these attitudes blocks assertive communication.

   The exception is that we tell people who are slow learners and people who might be victimized by strangers on the street NOT to make eye contact with strangers and to walk away from that person to prevent unsafe familiarity with potential offenders.

2. Saying "GOOD!"
   When a person has participated, respond with a heartfelt "Good!"
   "A good word does not cost more." [Yiddish proverb]

3. Smiling.
   A smile can be like sunshine to someone in the gloom.

4. Saying person's name.
   Remembering a person's name is a way of letting them know that we recognize them as an individual and care about them personally. Use name tags until you learn their names.

5. Paraphrasing or repeating what is said.

6. Touching.
   A gentle squeeze on the arm or a gentle pat on the back can be a healing, affirming connection.

Activity: Clapping Warm-Up:
Maturity level: All ages
To show unconditional appreciation from the group:

1. The leader asks enthusiastically, "How many of you know how to clap your hands?"
2. "OK, everyone, hold both of your hands in front of you, look at them. With the flat part of your hand hit the flat part of the other hand and listen to the sound you make."
3. "Now all together, let's clap."
4. "That was OK. Now let's make it even louder. That's better! Now, a louder clap; and let's add a smile to our faces as we clap! Good! Now, let's add a twinkle in our eyes, and a *yea* to our applause."

5. "Excellent! It feels wonderful for actors and performers to receive applause - like a zap of energy."
6. "We are going to get a chance to see what it's like to be a star and receive applause! I will go first." (The leader as role model receives applause with grace and gestures appreciation.) "Who wants to come up first?" When (name of person) comes up, smile, twinkle, say '*yea*' as you give him or her a big hand [hands clap] and zap!
7. The next participant comes up and gets zapped! ("Zap," from here on in refers to the leader or group giving an individual a lively round of applause.)
8. "Who wants to come up next?" Keep the pace moving. After many zaps, it's important that the leader be sensitive to the energy level and leave the activity before enthusiasm drops.
9. The leader says, "From now on, whenever anyone participates in the group, they will receive appreciation from us all by clapping."
10. Other methods of expressing appreciation may be utilized according to your group's physical abilities. Holding hands in the air, palms facing forward and waggling the wrists or fingers ("Tibetan applause") is quieter and is also effective. Stamping the feet works. Whatever system you choose, use it regularly and often.

UNCONDITIONAL APPRECIATION

Having the group applaud for each contribution is an effective way to reinforce expressing appreciation. This simple method of responding with positive reinforcement to any contribution to the group is a way of demonstrating that it's not what you say that is necessarily so important, but that you were willing to say it and contribute to the group. In other words, you don't have to be smart or answer questions with the so-called "right answers" to be appreciated. It is not anti-intellectual to bring a sense of caring and love into the group.

Activity: The Paraphrasing Game
Maturity level: Ages 7+
Make up open-ended questions and write them on index cards. All answers can be correct (*Feeling Good Playful Cards* are an excellent resource).
1. Form a circle of chairs.
2. Read Question Card to person on the left making eye contact (+smiling optional).
3. Paraphrase question to person on the left while making eye contact.
4. Listen carefully as the person on the left answers.
5. Paraphrase or repeat answer saying person's name and having eye contact.
6. While making eye contact ask person if your paraphrasing is what they meant.
7. If correct, make eye contact, smile, say "Good," and lead group in applause.
8. Next person on the left becomes leader for the person at their left, etc.

ATTITUDES TO DEVELOP

An important part of modeling attitudes is changing the way we communicate. If we use small words and talk down, we reinforce that position of inequity, of belittling those people. When we use sophisticated words followed by simpler words to clarify them, there is a sense of talking friend-to-friend rather than from high to low, and we are teaching new vocabulary at the same time.

As we see it, no one is better or worse than anybody else. We all have our lessons to learn and we all have lessons to teach. Our students teach us how to give and receive love. They are on a special mission to open our hearts to feel connected.

There are wealthy geniuses who don't know how to give or receive love; too arrogant or afraid to reach out, they are trapped in the belief that people are only with them for their money. Perhaps if they had a friend in special education, they could learn how to trust and love.

Some of us are learning to walk, some are learning appropriate behavior with others in public, some of us are learning to deal with fear, some of us are learning how to get along with our in-laws. We wish that we can get beyond the labels and get beyond the attitudes of limitation that we keep projecting on the people whom we label "developmentally disabled" or "mentally retarded." To get beyond those attitudes, it seems to us that each one of us is responsible for finding out who we really are.

If we identify ourselves only as a "professional" with the role of "helper," we may become attached to that role for our security. We then become attached to keeping the "helpless" helpless, so that we will continue to be needed. Who we really are (and who our clients really are) is not the role or the image or the label of who we think we are, or of who people said we were when we were growing up. Drop the attitudes of being above or below the people you are with. Only by cultivating an attitude and sense of equality can you and your students and co-workers create a safe environment that promotes unity and growth of potential.

Inside every one of us is a wise person. This is the silent observer that is available to us when we need to know what to do. We usually communicate with that part of us by being still and listening. Poets, philosophers and psychologists use different words to describe this inner guide. This part of us is able even if our bodies and/or minds are not. This wise person is also inside our so-called disabled clients. The more access we have to that place inside of us, the more we are able to connect to that similar wise person in our clients. It is from that inner, able place that the miracles occur. This may be one of the most important concepts to emphasize in special education.

A commonly believed self-esteem myth is: "If I don't feel good about myself, I cannot help others to feel good about themselves."

I believed that one for a long time. That belief is dead-ended. Whoever believes that may believe that there is no hope for them to help others to feel good.

It was really interesting how I found out it was a myth. One of my students was training to become a co-leader. This was a woman who had been in classes for slow learners all of her life.

Every morning she would raise her hand and ask: "Gloria, is it true that if you don't feel good about yourself, you can't help anybody else to feel good about themself?"

I would say: "Yes, Lois, that is true. And do you feel good about yourself?"

Lois would respond, "Sometimes I do and sometimes I don't." Then she would ask me, "Do you feel good about yourself, Gloria?"

And I would answer, "Well, sometimes I do and sometimes I don't." Then in the afternoon, Lois brought up the same question and we had the same conversation.

It took me about three months to finally realize that it was an illusion that I was the only teacher in my class. Lois and the people I served were really <u>my</u> teachers. They taught me what I really needed to know.

The reality can be:

> If you have the heartfelt intention to feel good about yourself and if you have the heartfelt intention to lift the spirits of those around you, then in healing you shall be healed. Act the way you would like to feel.

Perhaps the "slow learners'" mission is to play the role of the "helpless" so that we as the "helpers" can learn from them the fulfilling lessons of how to learn self-acceptance and how to give and receive love. Perhaps love is the only part of ourselves that really lasts forever.

If you are working in a situation where you wish to enhance the experience of others feeling good about themselves, you don't necessarily have to start off feeling good. You do have to act like you feel good, at least to get the energy going. In fact, you can just simply fake it. Reality soon overtakes you and you start to feel not just better but actually good!

One of the best ways to increase our own and others' feeling of self-worth is by enabling others to help themselves. This act of conscious kindness is one of the great missions of humankind. But helping someone else by doing something for them is not automatically a good thing. We can unintentionally sabotage their own growth and self-esteem that way.

AFFIRMATIONS

Without knowing it, through patterns of thought we create both affirmations and negations in our daily lives. For example, if you tell someone (or yourself) repeatedly, "I can't do anything right," that person or you may start to believe it; and then if it's reinforced in your environment as well as inside you, it becomes your reality. This can also be applied to building strengths. "I can do things for myself," reinforced with "You sure know how to get things done," makes for a positive experience. Try it. Before you go to sleep say "I will feel refreshed and happy in the morning" and believe it.

Participants are often more receptive to affirmations after a quieting and focusing activity like the voiced breathing exercises (described on page 34). Then the leader role models each affirmation by saying it in a way that sounds as if he or she really means it - in a firm but moderate and pleasant voice. The group repeats the affirmation. A useful exercise is for each member of the group to say the affirmation and then ask the group if it sounded as if he or she meant it. For instance, a participant may state "I feel good about myself" but grimace and shrug with a questioning tone of voice. The group can give feedback about the double message that is being communicated.

A variation to reinforce individuals in giving self-approval would be for one person to say an affirmation such as "I can be myself" and the group answers enthusiastically with "You can be yourself!" This is an especially useful technique when someone can use a positive zap from the group. Participants can make up their own affirmations and the group can repeat them back.

For people who are slow learners keep affirmations short, concise and simple. Follow difficult words with clarifiers. Use group approval techniques. Repeating affirmations takes about three to ten minutes per session and can become a worthwhile routine. Complete each affirmation session with sharing feelings and experiences of how it felt to say and hear them: "Which affirmations made you feel good? Which didn't? Did any bring up old memories or feelings?"

One time we were going around the circle in a class and each person said "I feel good about myself" and each person received appreciation through applause until we came to Alice. She started to say "I feel good..." but began to cry and said "I don't feel good about myself and I can't say it!"

We asked the group, "How many people here feel good about Alice?" Almost everyone in the group felt good about Alice and raised their hand and said "We feel good about you, Alice." Then Alice again attempted to say "I feel good about..." and again began to cry. We said to Alice, "Sometimes people don't feel good about themselves. That's OK. Say 'I feel good about myself' anyway and start getting used to it."

Then Alice said "I feel good about myself" about eight times, each time lightening up a bit, until a sparkle appeared in her eyes! Several weeks later we received a letter from Alice's teacher thanking us for giving Alice "permission" to feel good about herself. Alice didn't know it was OK to feel that way about herself.

Experiment with your own affirmations. Become aware of signs of strengths surfacing, and encourage their development.

For example, Bill was labeled "slow," and yet we noticed him remembering many things such as details and sequencing in the teaching process that everyone else seemed to forget. We would spontaneously say, "Bill has an excellent memory. He remembered to turn on the music at exactly the right time." We would refer to his successes during regular conversations as well as in class when Bill answered questions correctly. The rest of the group gradually referred to Bill's good memory as a matter of fact and so it <u>became</u> a fact and an asset to Bill's self-concept. And his memory for important details continues to amaze us!

Here is a list of some wonderful affirmations. We have collected them from a variety of sources and have included them so that you can use them in your classroom and even for your own personal use. The first ones are particularly useful with slow learners. The language of the rest of them may be more sophisticated, but you can change them to suit your needs. Make up your own as well.

Activity: Repeating affirmations
Maturity level: age 4+

Choose affirmations to fit individual verbal abilities. Write them on board or state them one at a time and ask class to repeat each one out loud.

1. I can pin my own name tag on.
2. I can do things for myself.
3. I feel good about myself.
4. I like myself.
5. I am happy to be alive.
6. I will be gentle with myself.
7. I can take good care of myself.
8. I am OK.
9. I love myself.
10. I am learning what I need.
11. I nurture and support myself.
12. I am good.
13. I enjoy a job well done.
14. I start each day with joy and energy.
15. I am here to help.
16. I am here to love.

17. I have a purpose here.
18. I know how to love.
19. I am not alone.
20. I can give and receive love.
21. I am loved.
22. God wants me to be happy.*

   *If use of the word "God" presents any concern at your facility, you might say:
   I am meant to be happy.

> **Refer to teens or adults by their adult names. This way you communicate that you really care about them as one adult to another adult.**

Activity: Name Tag Zap and Variations

With the student's consent, this is a good exercise to help change baby names to adult names. The group supports these decisions with acknowledgement and applause. For example, Chucky really preferred being called Chuck.

Note: Individuals may choose to give themselves a new name. If that is the case, encourage them to announce their decision themselves.

These activities are especially valuable with groups of people who are slow learners. We have used as co-leader a person who was himself labeled "retarded" but is now more independent and has been trained as a paraprofessional teacher. One of the best ways to increase self-esteem is by developing leadership skills. The following are specific objectives for learning:

1. To increase pride in one's name and one's self.
2. To change baby names to adult names if individual so chooses.
3. To develop leadership skills.
4. To develop confidence to act independently.
5. To reinforce concepts of male and female.
6. To increase appropriate participation in group activities.

Activity: Basic Introductory Name Tag Zap
   Maturity level: age 5+
1. Leader seats and quiets group.
2. Leader introduces the activity to the group, explaining that the purpose is to make everyone in the group feel appreciated.
3. Leader and co-leader demonstrate procedure by role-playing.
   a. Leader calls co-leader's name.
   b. Group "zaps" co-leader by clapping and saying, "Yea, (name of person)!"
   c. Co-leader comes up to receive name tag. The tag should look attractive.
   d. Leader pins tag on co-leader.
   e. Group zaps co-leader again.
   f. Co-leader sits down.
4. Leader then calls a student by their name tag name, and proceeds as just described.
5. Activity is completed when all students have received their name tags and received zaps from the rest of the group.

> Providing appropriate and achievable leadership roles is an important building block to self-esteem. When a student is given the chance to lead an activity that he or she <u>is</u> capable of performing successfully, there is immediate enhancement of self-esteem. Identifying these leadership skills is a valuable task for the teacher and the support group.

Variation Number 1: Student Leadership
In this variation, students assume leadership roles. Rather than sitting down after receiving their name tags, students remain standing, choose the next student's name tag, and lead the class in zapping that student.
1. Leader introduces activity.
2. Leader calls co-leader's name, and leads class in zapping co-leader.
3. Co-leader chooses a student's name, and leads class In zapping that student.
4. Co-leader sits down.
5. Student chooses another student, calls out that student's name, and leads class in zapping the student.
6. First student sits down; second student chooses another student, and leads a zap.
7. Activity continues as just described, and is completed when all have received name tags and zaps.

Variation Number 2: Using Students' Photos or Slides of Themselves
1. Leader shows a picture of a student and says, "Who is this?"
2. Class says that person's name.
3. Student whose photo was shown comes up for name tag.
4. Leader asks each person, "How do you like your picture?" "What do you see when you see yourself?" Ask group, "How do you like seeing (name of person)?"

Variation Number 3: Gender Identification
Students are told by leader which gender of student to call up next (i.e., to call either a male or a female.
1. Leader introduces and explains the activity, saying that each student will be told whether to call up a male or female next.
2. Leader reviews concept of gender. Leader asks all males to raise their hands. Leader reminds the class that males are also called boys or men, and that females are also called girls or women.
3. Leader begins activity by calling out co-leader's name, identifying him or her as a male or female, and zapping co-leader with applause.
4. Leader instructs co-leader to choose a male (or female) next.
5. Co-leader chooses a student, identifying him or her as a male or female, who receives name tag and zap.
6. Co-leader sits down. Leader tells student to choose a male (or female). Student chooses appropriate-gender student, and leads class in zapping him or her. Repeat until all students have their tags.
7. All students stand in a line. Each student is asked, "Are you a male or a female?"

Variation Number 4: "I Did It Myself"
In this variation, each student pins on his or her own name tag, and then says, "I did it myself."
1. Leader introduces the activity and variation. Leader explains that, this time, each student will have to pin on one's own name tag, and then proudly say to the class, "I

did it myself."
2. Leader and co-leader role model the activity.
3. Leader leads class in zapping co-leader.
4. Co-leader pins on his or her name tag.
5. Co-leader says, "I did it myself."
6. Leader and class zap co-leader.
7. Co-leader sits down. Leader calls up next student.
8. Student gets zapped by the class, pins on own name tag, says "I did it myself," gets zapped again, sits down. Repeat until all have name tags pinned on.

Variation Number 5: Using the Grab Bag
1. All name tags are placed in a bag, basket or box.
2. Leader introduces activity and explains that everyone's name tag is in the bag. Leader will choose a student to come up, reach into the grab bag, grab a name tag, read the name, and lead the class in zapping the student.
3. Leader stresses that if someone can't read a name, that person should say, "I need some help." Leader or another student will assist.
4. Leader and co-leader role model activity.
5. Co-leader chooses student by grabbing a tag from the bag, reading the name, and leading class in a zap.
6. Student reaches into bag, grabs a tag, reads the name, and leads class in a zap.
7. Repeat until all tags are distributed.

Activity: Removing Our Armor
   Maturity level: age 5+
We all go through life wearing a kind of armor for protection. Now, here in this safe place we don't need to protect ourselves so we can remove our armor with this guided touching activity. This is a symbolic activity as well as a practical opportunity for people who are rarely touched or who rarely have the opportunity to touch others, to do so appropriately.

First role-model the following:
1. The group is divided into pairs.
2. One person stands tall and straight while the other person places both hands on the top of the other person's head and lightly moves hands down the partner's body to the feet on the floor.
3. Shake out the hands to shake off the armor feeling.
4. Repeat these long continuous motions from head to foot, moving hands from above, then over the front, the sides, and the back of the partner's body. Point out that we respect the private parts of people's bodies. We don't touch female's breasts nor people's vaginas nor penises as we move our hands over their bodies. When finished, the person receiving "armor removal" tells how he or she feels (usually lighter). The one member of the pair thanks the partner and they switch roles.
5. With steady guidance, this exercise is one that nearly every student (including those who are severely retarded) can learn to do successfully.

The second self-esteem principle to keep in mind is:

> **The ongoing success of the participant is more important than predetermined goals, objectives or expectations. Acknowledge and build on successes and existing strengths.**

A leader must have a sense of direction on one hand, and must also be without goals on the other hand. The actual process, as it is happening, is probably the most significant and important goal.

A diagnostic practice widely accepted in educational circles is that we must first recognize someone's weaknesses or needs in order to design a plan of action to help them. These are called "needs assessments."

This is designed to build on what students or clients **don't** yet have. Some people call this "remediation." For example, if a student hates to read, we give him/her more to read. This can make the student fail. The failure confirms our initial diagnosis of his/her weakness. We must remember that what we have yet to learn is not necessarily our weakness. A better solution is to build confidence and skill using success and strength oriented approaches.

It is important to know what is needed but that isn't enough. How do you build on someone's "needs," something they don't have? Needs are lacks or absences. They are holes. You can't construct or build upon a hole as the foundation. You build on something solid, something that you already **have**. Doesn't it make more sense to create an inventory of people's strengths?

Tuning in to our own strengths is an on-going and life-long process. Many of our special strengths lay dormant until they are brought to life. Taking an inventory of the things we like about ourselves and others, things we like to do, interests, ways we like to act, and ways we like to be treated by others, will help to uncover the treasures of our own personal resources and self-respect. Such an inventory might include qualities like goodness, ability to forgive, caring for others, moral and physical strength, enthusiasm, creativity, sensitivity, sense of humor, understanding, gentleness, patience, will power and the potential for giving and receiving.

It has been said that contentment is not the fulfillment of what you want but the realization of how much you already have. To help you start tapping these individual strengths and resources use the following "Strength Assessments."

STRENGTH ASSESSMENT
"Things I Like To Do."

Maturity level: age 4+
This activity is an interview in which you utilize the self-esteem reinforcement techniques on page 13. For example, say "good," smile and say person's name after each response to the interview questions encouraging participation and rapport. Remember, **there are no wrong answers** to the strength assessment. **Adapt each session to the participant's attention span.**

STRENGTH ASSESSMENT
Things I Like To Do

1. What do you like best about school (job)? _____
2. What do you like to do when you come home from school (work)? _____
3. What do you do on weekends? _____
   church? _____ go visiting? _____ sleep? _____
4. What do you do at home? _____
   make your bed? _____ clean/dust? _____ cook? _____
5. What is your favorite outdoor activity? _____
6. What is your favorite movie? _____ TV Program? _____
7. Who is your favorite friend? _____ Relative? _____
8. What is your favorite song? _____ Music? _____
9. What do you like to do best? _____
   2nd best? _____
   3rd best? _____

After they have answered the questions (or some of the questions) and you have filled in this questionnaire, you say: "(Person's name), let me tell you what I have learned about you, and you nod your head if I heard you right. OK?"

Note: Even if the participant's answers aren't to your liking, accept them enthusiastically with an attitude of unconditional appreciation.

EXAMPLES OF THE STRENGTH ASSESSMENT FEEDBACK:
1. "George, I learned that what you like best about your job is lunch break. Is that right? Good."
2. "When you come home from work, George, you like eat and watch TV."
3. "On week-ends you enjoy riding in the car and visiting your Uncle Joe."
4. "At home you make your own bed and help cook. Is that right?"

Keep a chart of each person's strengths for future group activities and reinforce those strengths.

Ex: Develop leadership skills by encouraging participants to teach you their favorite song, share their favorite music, or help someone cook or teach a skill, or talk about a favorite television program.

DEVELOPING AN "INDIVIDUAL EDUCATIONAL PLAN" (IEP)

A team approach is best for recognizing and reinforcing individual strengths as well as identifying and addressing an individual's most noticeable characteristics that indicate low self-esteem.
    The following samples of "Individual Educational Plans" will guide staff members, parents and paraprofessionals in developing a collaborative approach to addressing self-esteem, socialization and strengths.

PREPARING YOUR STAFF TO CREATE IEPs
    Before meeting with the staff regarding IEPs, teach the basic self-esteem principles and the techniques to reinforce self-esteem. Also, take each member of your staff through the Yes-No Process (on page 32). The Yes-No Process is a core activity that each staff member needs to learn. They will find it a lifesaver when their clients' (and/or their own) anger gets to be unmanageable.
    In the following examples of Individual Educational Plans, questions 1, 2 and 3 can be answered with the entire team, including parents and paraprofessionals brainstorming together. For question 1, everyone is asked to focus on one client or student and list the characteristics of that individual that indicate low self-esteem, especially in terms of what they need in order to enhance their self-esteem. This approach focuses the group into a proactive, situation-solving direction. For question 2, list the client/student's strong points. Number 3, invite suggestions for what might be done to give recognition to those strengths, taking into consideration the client/student's self-esteem needs. At the following meeting, each staff member states what they will do to implement step number 4, what they will do to help change how the student/client feels about her/himself.
    The Individual Educational Plan shown below is geared toward self-esteem. It can also be adapted to address social or sexual issues/problems. For example, number one could say: "List the characteristics that indicate inappropriate social or sexual behavior." These characteristics should be chosen to reflect what the client/student may need. For example, if the response to #1 were to state: "inappropriate touching private

body parts in class," then #3 might state: "needs to learn that touching private parts is done in private locations only." Number 4 would ask: "Steps that staff members (or parents) will take to help client/student change inappropriate social or sexual behavior," and the staff members would indicate how they will implement these changes. One response might be: "When client/student is observed touching his/her private parts in class, I will say 'That's for private, where no one can see you. This is a public place where everyone can see you'." Another response might be: "I will schedule a 'Public & Private' teaching exercise for next month's workshop meeting." [The Public & Private exercise is found on page 29 of this Guide.]

Self-esteem is the priority at this time and all of the good work you do will act as a foundation for addressing problems having to do with social or sexual issues.

By identifying and using individual strengths as a foundation to their ongoing success you can work on the needs of your students and clients while building their self-esteem more effectively.

INDIVIDUAL EDUCATION PLAN for Client: _____

1. List this individual's most noticeable characteristics that indicate low self-esteem.
    a, b, c, etc.

2. What are this person's strong points?
    a, b, c, etc.

3. What might be done to give recognition to these strengths?
    a, b, c, etc.

4. Steps that staff members will take to help client to feel good about herself:
    a. Staff Member: _____ will
        1, 2, 3 etc.

    b. Staff Member: _____ will
        1, 2, 3 etc.

    c. Staff Member: _____ will
        1, 2, 3 etc.

Four model Individual Educational Plans are shown in Appendix A (page 121).

PARENTS' ACTIONS ENHANCING THEIR CHILDREN'S SELF-ESTEEM
We have found these suggestions useful as points of reference:
1. Address your young adult son/daughter with adult names (Bob rather than Bobby; Sue rather than Suzie).
2. Include your son/daughter in conversations:
    a. Make eye contact.
    b. Listen to what your son/daughter has to say; giving time for your son/daughter to say it. Encourage your son/daughter to speak for themselves.
    c. Give feedback to what your son/daughter has to say.
    d. Include your son/daughter in decision making - respect decisions and allow them to make mistakes.

3. Reinforce strengths - showing appreciation for tasks well done.
4. Encourage and listen to expression of needs and preferences. Encourage assertiveness.
    a. Include your son/daughter in responsibilities in the home.
    b. Use regular vocabulary followed up by clarifiers. Example: "What do you prefer? What do you want?"
    c. Allow for private place and time.
    d. If your son or daughter is ready, provide opportunities for them to be home alone and to go out alone.
    e. Support social interaction and varied leisure time activities and interests
    f. Encourage your son/daughter to choose own wardrobe - with guidelines toward appropriate dress and hairstyles.
    g. State what is appropriate behavior rather than drawing attention to inappropriate behavior. (Example: If you are correcting a client/student who inappropriately hugs whomever they greet, say: "It's better to shake hands when you greet someone".)

TEACHING PEOPLE WHO ARE SLOW LEARNERS

WHAT ARE THEIR NEEDS?

People who are diagnosed and labeled as being "mentally retarded" are unique individuals. And they are also like other people. Like all of us, they need balance in their lives between **work** (having a sense of mission), **fellowship** (friendly relationships with others), **solitude** (privacy) and **intimacy** (personal loving relationship with another or with a group). Once we learn what their special needs are and provide for them, then we can address their normal aspects, the parts that they share with the rest of humanity so that they (and we) can grow beyond labels.

To improve the quality of life for people with disabilities, mainstreaming laws, socialization programs, independent living programs, independent learning programs, and now an awareness of the need for self-esteem programs and support groups, are being developed to prepare people to succeed as members of society. The intention of mainstreaming is to provide a sense of belonging, of inclusion in our society for people who have previously been excluded.

Why bother? Is this just to be nice? One purpose is actually to reduce the amount of care that these citizens will require by enabling them to take more care of themselves. For example, if we want immigrants to join our society as contributors and not as liabilities, we teach them the rules so that they can learn to succeed. In the same way, mainstreaming, socialization programs and information programs (that include academic skills, behavior awareness and sexual knowledge) are designed to enable citizens with disabilities to catch up on what they missed in their regular schooling. With this assistance they will be able to participate in conventional society more effectively as contributors, as companions and friends, as teachers, as workers and even as taxpayers. Some don't achieve this right away. Many do when they are provided with compassionate and effectively taught information. And then, living becomes much simpler not only for persons with disabilities but for those around them who no longer have to take care of them but instead can coexist and work *with* them.

Of perhaps even greater importance is the prevention of problems, especially those of victimization. People are often concerned about victimization of so-called "normal" people by people who look and act differently. They may be scared of strange behaviors. What is in fact more common is that people with learning and physical disabilities are victimized by so-called "normal" members of society. They appear to be trusting easy prey and are actually robbed, injured and raped more often than almost any other segment of our population. Since they don't always tell us about it, we are not always made aware of these problems.

When you as a teacher or parent are working on developing community support for a curriculum in self-esteem, social skills and sexual information for people with disabilities, it may be wise to approach the process of encouraging mainstreaming with these preventive measures in mind.

GAINING SUPPORT

Since we need to create a safe, supportive environment in which to provide socialization education and training, it is logical to enlist the support of parents and the community in this process. We find that more support is received when you approach parents with a view that does not focus so much on sexuality as much as it does on the **whole** person in a society. Speak to your audience by saying things like, "I am interested in your son or daughter feeling good about themselves, getting to know themselves, becoming more independent and making appropriate decisions."

In our own work, we present the concepts of self-esteem enrichment, social skill enrichment, and concerns and facts about preventing sexual exploitation. We teach that there are public and private body parts and public and private touching. We teach the difference between strangers and friends. We stress that our body is our own and that if someone wants to touch our private body parts or asks us to touch their private parts, we can say "no" and mean it. We discuss the consequences of going off with a stranger and we role-play how people's sons and daughters can protect themselves by saying "no" and walking away. We discuss specific people each student would be able to go to if there were a problem, and how to ask for help even if they are told that it must be kept a secret. An important principle to remember is that if a student comes to you for help, be certain that the student knows that he or she is not to blame and will be protected from the offender. If you are uncomfortable dealing with the situation, find someone appropriate who can protect the student without blame.

In the "Sexual Exploitation Kit" by Seattle Rape Relief[*] it was noted that assaults are not perpetrated only by strangers: "Handicapped persons are most often sexually exploited by people they know. A high percent of all handicapped victims who reported to Seattle, Washington Rape Relief were sexually exploited by friends, acquaintances, caretakers and relatives. These are often people who would be least suspect. Sex offenders, like victims, are individuals of all ages, races, social and economic backgrounds."

We also explain to parents that we teach that if their sons and daughters attempt to touch someone else's private parts without permission, they can be arrested and put into prison. One special education teacher was heartbroken when her naïve Special Ed student was arrested, thrown into jail, had his head shaven and was labeled forever as a sex offender for touching a ten-year-old girl on the bus. He told his teacher that he didn't know he could get into trouble if he touched a child (this is described on page 54). He was lonely and didn't have the social skills to make verbal contact.

---

[*] Seattle Rape Relief closed its doors in 1999. It's former volunteers opened a new organization called Communities Against Rape and Abuse (CARA).

Exploitation and victimization often result from the lack of social knowledge. When the program is presented in a positive manner, parents gain confidence and support the purpose of the program.

Invite the parents to share with you their views concerning potentially controversial issues such as masturbation, dating, marriage, sexual intercourse, responsibility, independence, birth control, abortion and sterilization to become aware of their beliefs and values. This is an opportunity to educate, clarifying misconceptions, myths and fears by presenting factual information about bodily functions that are already in effect in their sons and daughters. Not talking about things that are already happening leads to easy victimization by so-called smarter people who *do* know what's happening. When someone understands what is happening in recognizing sexually exploitive situations and what to do about it (like saying "no" firmly and walking away), that person is better protected and can better prevent problems from developing. If a problem should develop, the person can recognize it as a problem and is equipped to talk about it with a responsible adult such as a parent or counselor.

When you present a program such as this, attuned to the whole person, it is much more acceptable than a presentation stressing sexuality alone. It has balance to it. We think that what upsets so many people about a sexuality program is that, sometimes, the program addresses only the awkward mechanical aspects of sex - just the genitals. When it is brought into perspective and into balance with other aspects of living such as the privileges and responsibilities of adulthood, then it becomes a program that parents and communities respect and want.

TEACHING ENVIRONMENT

The first step is to create a safe, supportive environment where people can be together and feel secure and express themselves without feeling judged or compared. No put-downs are allowed. We communicate with positive terms. If someone makes a mistake or does something wrong, present the appropriate behavior. This is a time and a place where we can rehearse for activities of social living. We do this by providing a safe place where everyone is involved and actively participates. We have no observers in our group. When visitors come to see what we do, they too participate. Thus we create a supportive place for everybody where they can rehearse actual social situations. For example, you can practice how to say hello to someone of the opposite sex that you have just met. You can practice how to ask someone to dance or to go out on a date. In response, there is a group of people that claps and says, "You can do it, you are really good!" Then that person can go out and feel more confident approaching these situations in real life.

APPROPRIATE LANGUAGE

Talking down to people who are slow learners doesn't work. Use language that is understandable and listen to yourself as you speak. When you do use words that may be unfamiliar to your class, use them in context and follow them with explanatory words that can be readily understood. Then repeat the words. "Baby" language is inappropriate when you are attempting to prepare people for adulthood. To refer to a 55-year-old man who may be slow to learn as "Jimmy" usually reflects the fact that his teachers or attendants think of him and treat him as a child. It is not uncommon in our groups, after they have been meeting for a few months, that a client may select a new name for himself or herself. We always support that choice, because it usually reflects an enhanced self-concept.

REPETITION OF CORRECT ANSWERS

When you ask a comprehension question and the student doesn't know the answer, don't make them feel wrong or judged; give the correct answer and then repeat the process if necessary. For example, when you ask, "Jane, are you a male or a female?" you are teaching the concept of sex differences and identity and teaching the words *male* and *female*. Jane doesn't understand or doesn't know the answer. You would say, "Jane, you are a female, a woman. Now tell me, are you a male or a female?" "Female." "Very good, Jane. You are a female." Of course, this will probably be repeated many more times during the next several days or even months. But, remember, this is not a lesson with right and wrong answers. This kind of teaching to people who are slow at learning requires lots of repetition. Reinforce correct responses immediately: "Jane got that right! Jane knows that she is a female. You did that very well, Jane!"

Students who are slow learners need lots of varied, simple repetitions but without the process becoming boring. This requires some creativity on the part of the teacher. Concepts to be repeated can be emphasized at different times and opportunities during each day. Varying the pace of the lesson between high-energy participatory activities and low-key less active times is effective.

GENERALIZATIONS

People who are slow learners are usually not good at generalizing information or applying abstract concepts. Teaching by analogy is not usually effective. We've found that it is not a good idea to assume that because something has been explained and taught in one setting, it will be remembered and performed appropriately in another setting. For example, we use role-playing quite often in teaching. One situation we practice a great deal is saying "no" to a stranger.

"What do you say when a stranger offers you a ride in his car? You say 'no,' and walk away. What do you do when a stranger approaches you on the sidewalk and says, 'Come with me into the alley'? You say 'no,' and you walk away."

This may sound good in class, but must be tested outside. If the student doesn't say "no" and walk away from a stranger in a test that you have set up for her/him in public, that means that she/he still needs supervision (see page 46).

We found that in teaching the concepts of private and public, we couldn't assume that our students would generalize or apply those guidelines. For instance, that reading an adult magazine is not appropriate in a public place, or that a private place isn't just where you can't see other people, but a place where other people cannot see you.

RELATING TO OTHERS
SOCIAL BEHAVIOR

APPROPRIATE BEHAVIOR

Students who are slow learners need to know what "normal" behavior is and they need to have a safe place with trusted people around where they can rehearse plans to live in a "normal" world. Video feedback is extraordinarily valuable for people to see how they appear to others and learn how they can improve their behavior, including their body language, dress and communication skills. As they begin to *appear* more appropriate, they act and feel more appropriate.

They need to recognize what behaviors are considered inappropriate without themselves being identified as inappropriate people.

> Before giving feedback, always give first chance to the person who is being corrected to offer a more appropriate way to handle his or her own situation. This empowers them to learn more independence from their own mistakes and provides a role model for self-improvement.
>
> If someone's participation is inappropriate, do not put attention on reinforcing the inappropriate behavior and their being wrong. Present the appropriate behavior with enthusiasm to provide guidance in the appropriate direction. Say: "What would be a better way to do/say that?"

This approach does not focus on shaming and making someone feel wrong and less worthy but rather provides clear direction. You may comment on someone's inappropriate behavior by describing the consequences of the inappropriate behavior and then describe a better way to say or do something.

For example, a student in my class would punch the social worker's door whenever he was angry. I first asked, "What happens when you punch the door in?" He answered, "I get into trouble and have to use the little money I have to fix the door." I asked, "What is a better way to show your anger?" We then brainstormed other better ways for him to express anger and found that hitting a pillow worked better.

By participating in helping others *to help and appreciate themselves,* we leave them stronger and more independent.

Here are two stories to share and discuss:

Three of us had gone to a restaurant for lunch. When we were leaving, the waitress came running out and angrily grabbed Jim by the shoulder. While we were leaving the restaurant he had seen money on some empty tables. He picked up the money and put it in his pocket. We explained, "People leave money on tables when they leave restaurants as a tip for their waitresses. That money belongs to the waitress. If you take that money it's called stealing and you can be put in jail if you steal tips left on restaurant tables." I then asked Jim what happened next and what he had learned. He proudly reported that he put the tips back where they belong and would never do that again, and "no one should ever steal tips."

We were in a restaurant last week and a family came into the restaurant and sat down at a table. All of a sudden everybody in the restaurant began to stare at the boy who was with the family. He looked normal but he was doing something that was inappropriate. Everybody in the restaurant looked at him and stopped eating. I asked the group, "Do you know why they were staring at him?" The group guessed it: "Because he spoke too loudly in the restaurant. And you're supposed to speak softly in a restaurant."

Just as a self-esteem program for adolescents must point out how normal we all are, how everyone goes through puberty with all its complex and confusing changes, so too a socialization program must identify what behavior is appropriate and what is not normal or appropriate.

PUBLIC AND PRIVATE

Maturity level: all ages

The most dramatically inappropriate types of behavior are usually those that have to do with or suggest sexual activity. This includes sexual activity with oneself such as masturbation, or with another including the entire spectrum from public exposure to touching another to having sexual intercourse. The most valuable teaching guideline for defining appropriate behavior is the understanding of public and private places, and public and private parts of the body.

When teaching this concept for your group or client, keep the rules simple:

> Rule 1: Private parts of the body are for private places.
> Rule 2: Public parts of the body are for public places.

A private place is where no one can see you. A public place is where there can be other people around. The private parts of the body are those parts that we keep covered with our underwear. For females: breasts, buttocks, pubic area (vulva, vagina); for males: buttocks, pubic area (penis, scrotum). The public parts of the body are those parts that are exposed. Private parts of the body may be touched when we are in private places. Public parts of the body may be touched when we are in public. With this simple system it is possible to deal with a whole host of problems and situations that commonly arise with people who are slow learners.

If someone is touching or exposing a private part of their body, simply offer the reminder: "That's a *private* part of your body and this is a *public* place where people can see you. *Private* touching is for a *private* place where nobody can see you." This means that a private place must be available so that appropriate touching behavior is possible.

PUBLIC AND PRIVATE PARTS OF THE BODY

This card game is a playful way of making sure that each student knows which parts of his or her body are public (and what that means) and which parts are private (and what that means).

The following are specific objectives for learning:
1. To teach and evaluate participants' understanding of public and private body parts and public and private places.
2. To facilitate discussion about private body parts and private places.

Activity: Card Game for Public and Private Parts of the Body
1. Make a set of index cards with a name and/or a picture (sketch or photograph) of individual body parts, one to each card. Include face, shoulders, hands, feet, vagina, penis, buttocks, breasts, etc. (in some societies, the hair, or the face or the feet are considered private parts and are not for public display).
2. Prepare two boxes, one marked "public," one marked "private."
3. Seat group in a circle.
4. Taking turns, each participant takes a card and:
    a. identifies name of the body part.
    b. identifies body part on his or her own body or points to same body part on large wall chart or drawing on wall (Body Tracing Activity, page 86).
5. Leader reminds participants, "The private parts are the parts we keep covered."
6. Participant then places card in the "public" or "private" box; or group votes which box in which each card belongs.

Activity: Pictures of Public and Private Places
1. Have ready a variety of photographs or pictures from newspapers and magazines, including stores, theaters, restaurants, living rooms, bathrooms, kitchens, bedrooms, parks, swimming pools, etc. If possible, include photos of students' own bedrooms and bathrooms.
2. Show the pictures one by one and ask the group to identify each place as being either public or private. Or, taking turns, each participant selects a picture and identifies it as either a public or a private place. Point out that "a private bedroom in someone else's house is not a private place for you."
3. Stress that private places such as your bedroom or bathroom should have the door closed. If the bedroom is shared with someone else, the private place is under the covers. No one else can see you. That is what makes it private.
4. Discussion: Apply these public/private rules of appropriate behavior to other situations.
    Where is an appropriate place to ....?:
    a. read a Playboy Magazine, or a magazine with pictures of naked people? On a bus? At the dinner table? At a party? On a date? At your job? At school? In your bedroom? In the bathroom?
    b. scratch an itch on your private parts?
    c. pick your nose? (Do you keep a tissue or handkerchief in your pocket or purse?)
    d. expelling gas (burping, passing flatus).
    e. smell your armpit?
    f. put on deodorant?
    g. change your clothing? Take off your shoes and socks?
    h. floss your teeth?
    i. talk about private subjects like body functions, sex, other people, having your period, wet dreams, using swear words?
    j. talk about private thoughts (things you think about that you don't want everyone, the public or your parents, to know)?

Privacy has been a problem for most people growing up, whether disabled (intellectually or physically) or not. With the door closed, the bathroom or the bedroom (under the covers) is usually available and appropriate for private touching of oneself. Institutions with public restrooms and dormitories may need to have doors installed where needed to create private space. Some institutions need to set up a special private room that residents or clients can use and be appropriate for private touching of oneself.

If a resident is touching his private parts, the staff can simply say, "That's for the private room, this is in public where everyone can see you," and then guide him to the appropriate place without embarrassment.

SEX INFORMATION FOR STUDENTS WHO ARE SLOW LEARNERS

All people, not only disabled people, need to understand their own bodies and their body parts, and understand what normal growth, (including physical, mental and emotional), is all about. In this way they can interpret their growth changes into adulthood as being normal. Teenagers who are fortunate will have resources from which to draw accurate information. These sources include parents, teachers, friends, TV, movies and books. Even when some of the specific information is not accurate, especially information acquired from "the street," these bits of data get to be fitted into the overall store of information acquired and can be corrected as more information becomes available. People who are slow learners usually lack this wide diversity of resources and so it becomes all the more important that the information they do receive from us, their teachers, be most accurate and comprehensible to them.

One young teenager who was a slow learner had just started menstruating. No one had informed her that all women have periods and she interpreted her monthly bleeding as punishment. She thought she was going to die from the bleeding. She buried her soiled underwear, fearful of being found out as being different than other people.

If this young woman had an informed, askable friend or relative she could consult without fear, she could have enjoyed the feelings and knowledge of becoming a woman, of becoming an adult like other people she looked up to. She would have had a new self-concept to build upon, feeling more in common with the rest of the human species. Wouldn't it have made a difference if she had someone who taught her what to expect from her normal development? They could have used this opportunity to affirm a new beginning and bonding with other women. "How wonderful! You are becoming a woman. You are blossoming into a beautiful more independent woman!"

From this foundation of commonality, she (and all of us) can build healthy and enabling self-concepts. We build on what we have in common, as well as our individual uniquenesses, and then we get to share experiences of success.

Outlines for teaching specific sexual information are presented in later parts of this book. The methods for teaching this material are essentially the same for those who are slow learners as they are for people with other disabilities. More repetition is required. Consistent use of simple words is required. Even after something is learned, it must be reviewed and described again, months later. The slide curriculum, *Life Horizons* by Winifred Kempton, is especially valuable. Occasionally, when embarrassing moments arise during a sex education class, the group may dissolve into a mass of whoops and hollerings, along with much laughter. There's nothing wrong with that. If you remember to use the unconditional-appreciation applause activity when people contribute to the group, that applause can refocus the group.

THE YES-NO PROCESS:
PREPARATION FOR DECISION MAKING

BACKGROUND

I developed the Yes-No Process when I was teaching a class at a sheltered workshop for adults with developmental disabilities. Many of the clients seemed to be walking around with a lot of tension in their bodies. Their fists or jaws were often held clenched and it appeared that they seemed to be saying "no" with their bodies even if they were saying "yes" with the words they spoke.

We had been discussing sex in our class when a 29-year-old blind woman came up to me afterwards to tell me that during break times from the workshop she and another client were having sexual intercourse behind the liquor store across the street and that she didn't want this to happen. But the way she said it was, "Well, I don't want it to happen anymore," in an unconvincing, little girl's voice.

I asked her, "What did you tell him (the other client) when he started to touch your private parts?"

She said, "Well, I told him I wanted to wait until we got married and then maybe we could have sex," again in the voice of a very shy little girl.

I asked her, "Did you say 'no'?"

"Well I think so."

"How did you say 'no'?"

She answered in a child's voice, with a rising inflection at the end, as in a question:

"No?"

I said, "Say it like you really, <u>really</u> mean it!"

Again the questioning: "No?"

We spent considerable time on learning to say "no" in that class. We noticed how many other people at the workshop would say "no" with a questioning sound to it, as if they were seeking approval.

In normal development, children go through a stage when they seem to say nothing else but "no" and that is part of their own assertion that they are individuals. The "no" stage is actually the "I am" stage.

Until you can say "no" adequately, you can't really say "yes" and mean it. This is the beginning of the whole process of decision making. Many of the people who are developmentally disabled have their decisions made for them as they are growing up because it is assumed that they don't know enough to decide things for themselves.

It may be that when they went through their "no" stage, they were not adequately acknowledged.

When we introduced the Yes-No Process at the workshop we brought out that unexpressed "no" and incredible things began to happen. People changed their names. People who never spoke started talking. The process is designed for nonverbal people as well. If you can breathe, you can do the Yes-No Process.

A man named Bill was in our class. He rarely spoke. Several months after he started participating in the Yes-No Process, his mother related this story to me. She was getting ready to go out shopping with Bill. She asked him if he wanted to come along. He said, "no!" very clearly and assertively. Bill had never said "no" to going out shopping before. I asked her how she felt about him saying "no." She was completely surprised but she also liked hearing him take a firm stand. She said to him that he didn't have to go since he didn't want to. Shortly thereafter he decided to go. His mother noticed a definite change in his behavior because he had asserted himself and succeeded, so that when he did go shopping, it was his choice to do so.

Sometime during the next month he changed his name to Robert. His family supported that change. He insisted that everyone at the workshop call him Robert. They did. In a certain sense, he created himself anew. He had been practically nonverbal and now he had not only chosen a new name for himself but had also made sure everyone around him used his new name. He started to relate to other people and in fact he gained a girlfriend. They held hands. He became more verbal with her and with others. He became more helpful at his job. It was a fantastic change!

Jane was another client at the workshop. Although she was 30 years old she looked 16 and most people called her Janie. Jane never spoke but she did like to behave as though she did by whispering. She would often come up to me and whisper in my ear, "Spsspsspss."

I had a private session with her shortly after I had taught the Yes-No Process. She came into the room and in a partly playful and partly serious way she started to shout "no" to me. Then she came toward me and hit me. I watched this with some amazement because she had never done anything like that before. When she hit me (and it wasn't hard) I moved with the blow and fell to the ground. Jane was horrified. She had never before made anyone fall to the ground. As a matter of fact she had hardly made anything happen before. Then she saw me laughing and she started to smile. She got down beside me and started to mother me. She cradled my head, snapped my shirt snaps, buttoned my jacket buttons and helped me to get up. This is someone whose mother does everything for her - dresses her, takes her everywhere and even buttons her buttons. Here, Jane was acting as my mother and I was loving it.

Several days later Jane came up to me to whisper in my ear. I expected to hear the usual, "spsspsspss," but instead heard something like, "There's going to be a fire this afternoon." It was like hearing a ghost! I thought: when someone who never talks says that there's going to be a fire, I'd better tell someone about this! I went running to the Education Director and said to her, "You won't believe this, but it's as if the dead have risen! Jane spoke to me and said there is going to be a fire this afternoon!"

The Education Director said, "Holy smokes! Jane must have overheard people in the staff room discussing that someone was going to be fired this afternoon!" Jane was always permitted in the staff room because she was nonverbal. It "paid off" for her to be nonverbal. She enjoyed extra privileges not accorded to others who could talk. Somehow, the empowerment of the Yes-No Process had brought out her own abilities to express herself.

These exercises are for use with students/clients and their parents/guardian when you are introducing the curriculum. Use them with other teachers in your school/facility to demonstrate assertiveness training.

TEACHING THE YES-NO PROCESS

Activity: Learning How to Say "No" and "Yes" - and Mean It
Maturity level: age 4+

The following are specific objectives for learning:
1. To reduce tensions that may precede certain topics of discussion.
2. To exercise neglected muscles, especially for sedentary people.
3. To prepare to say "no" and "yes" and mean it.

4. To provide a structure for teaching deep, sustained breathing patterns.
5. To liven everyone up.
6. To improve awareness of breathing patterns to promote clearer, smoother, flowing speech. (ex: reducing tensions in the throat.)
7. To gain awareness of proper posture for full breathing.
8. To experience vocalization in unison.
9. To promote a sense of group participation.
10. To share a common experience.
11. To provide a structure in which to experience one's vocal power.
12. To provide tools for expressing "no" and "yes" with strength and meaning.
13. To promote a sense of self-power and one's own identity in learning basic communication skills.
14. To promote a sense of ableness and assertiveness.
15. To provide tools for expressing feelings like anger and joy.

How do we know if someone is alive? One way is to find out if he or she is breathing. Our breathing is our connection to our life force, to our aliveness. We all tend to diminish or stop breathing without even realizing it when we experience tension, suspense, worry, or fear. Natural deep breathing is an effective way to relax and feel comfortable with ourselves. Many persons with physical deformities, or who have other disabilities, may have serious impediments to adequately deep respirations. Scoliosis, muscular dystrophy and wheelchair patients are special beneficiaries of pulmonary exercises. Breathing together is a useful and safe way for a group to perform an activity together, to feel closer with one another. Here are five different ways to breathe together:

BREATHING AND BREATHING AWARENESS
Sit down on a firm chair, feet flat on the floor (including people in a wheelchair), legs not crossed, back straight. You want to wake up everyone. Get the whole person involved. We will use breathing, moving, voicing, expressing. This is a wonderful activity to do together. Aside from its intended purpose, it is an active way of being together. Everyone in the room at the time, including other teachers, parents, aides or observers, participate together.
1. Voiced Breathing: "Everyone breathe *in* through your nose and fill your lungs with as much air as you can hold. Breathe *out* through your mouth. Let your jaws relax into a partly open position. As you exhale, make a continuous voiced sound (aaaahhhh, oooohhhh or aaaauuuum). Fill the room with your sound." Inhale through the nose and exhale through the mouth with the voiced sound as a group for ten minutes or longer.
2. Everyone stands in a circle. "Plant your feet firmly on the ground about one or two feet apart with knees slightly bent. Give yourself a good, solid base to stand on. Feel as if you are grabbing the earth with your toes… as if you are a tree and your toes are your roots. No one can knock you over now. You are rooted in the ground."
3. Then say, "Breathe in through your nose, filling your lungs as before. Push the air down inside you to your belly. Now as you breathe out, make a sharp, quick, low-pitched sound, like a vigorous grunt. Keep your mouth open as you make this sound." Demonstrate this. Do it together. Then do it one by one with each client. Use positive feedback to encourage everyone. It doesn't matter if it's not done well. Cheer everyone on each time. You may be repeating this exercise for weeks or months, so give everyone time. Encourage everyone to clap after each client's expression. Everyone enjoys giving support and everyone enjoys receiving support.

4. Stand in the circle with your feet planted securely and your knees slightly bent. Do the same inhales and exhales as before. This time, punctuate the exhaled sound or grunt with a vigorous downward "karate chop" with one or both hands. Use the whole arm and shoulders to do this. Do it vigorously and dramatically, as if in the movies. This "chop" adds the power of movement to the voiced sound.
5. Continue the process by adding a different hand motion. This time, as you inhale, bring your arms up with the fists clenched, and then as you exhale releasing the sound, bring your fists down forcefully in a hitting action. You don't actually strike anything.
6. The next process is to change the grunt into a vigorous statement of "no." Bring the "no" up from the very deepest, lowest part of your belly. At first, you'll be going around the circle, one by one, giving each participant the chance to make the voiced sound and the movement individually, as well as following it with the group doing it all together. And you'll be encouraging everyone with lots of positive feedback ("Great, Jim, that was really good! Mary - wonderful! Sally…, didn't Sally do a great job? Really good!") and clapping and cheering.
7. Then, as the group is finishing this "no" process, turn on some lively music. (We use a tape of "La Bamba.") "Everyone shake your hands; shake your elbows; shake your shoulders; shake your heads," etc. "Dance! Shake out the 'no' tension in your body. As you shake, rejoice with 'yes'! Say it. Call it out. Yes to you! Yes to me! Yes to moving! Yes to breathing! Yes to being me! Yes to life!"

Now everyone is livened up and feeling strong and present. The more clearly we express our "no," the more clearly we can express our "yes."

The "I Can Say 'NO!'" filmstrip and cassette (by the authors, transferred to DVD) demonstrates the "Yes-No Process". See Resource List for details.

Activity: Pillow-Hitting, Saying "No!"
Maturity level: age 4+

The same process of coming down with clenched fists and saying "no," can be carried further to release anger, fear, hostility and negativity and to make room for feelings of joy, relief, connectedness and well being. *Like* everyone else, your client or son or daughter may have received many mixed messages and rejection from the world around him or her. *Unlike* everyone else, this person may have far fewer opportunities to express that anger, resentment, hostility, to say "no" instead of "OK" or "yes" as is so often the requirement. Here's a chance to express and release that unstated "no"!

The group can sit around in a circle. "Anyone mad? Someone bug you? Anyone angry? Here's how we can get it out."
1. "Sit down on your knees and put a big pillow in front of you. Take a deep breath in through your nose as you rise up on your knees, arms overhead with clenched fists. Then bring your fists and arms down along with your shoulders and your back and the rest of your body coming along."
2. When you repeat this activity with your group and get to the part where you say: "Take a deep breath in through your nose…," have the group say it along with you: "Breath in…,"
3. Leader says: "Now exhale through your mouth and vocalize 'no' (or an alternative sound or grunt) as your fists strike the pillow." Students may use other words besides "no" such as "I hate you," or "I hate it when I have to…," or "I won't let you control what I do," etc. for unexpressed anger or other negative feelings.
4. Leader and group respond: "Good! Breathe in…"

5. Repeat #2: Student hits pillow on exhale, expresses anger: "No, no, no, *no!*" and repeats as often as needed.
6. After each exhale and expression of "no" or other word, the group responds with: "Good! Breathe in…"
7. The person hitting the pillow decides when he or she is finished and then receives expressed appreciation from the group.
8. It is essential to continue repeating the process until the person hitting the pillow is clearly finished.

> *During a session one client had so much pent up anger that I felt frightened that I would lose control of him and that I had opened "Pandora's Box." I feared that all his pent up feelings would lead to violence against the whole group and me. I stopped him before he was finished. When I looked into his eyes he appeared gone and in a daze. I realized that I needed to allow him to finish so I positioned myself behind him and raised his hands up over his head, getting him back into the pillow hitting, breathing rhythm of saying "no," and he took over his process. Our group supported him with "Breathe in…" and after each vocalization (on his exhale) and pillow hitting, we said, "Good."*
>
> *We continued with him until he felt finished. It took about twenty minutes until he was exhausted but cleared of his burden. He looked at all of us and said, "Now I'm finished." We saw a peace in his eyes that was never there before. He felt good and we were all happy that we could be there for him.*
>
> *Rather than "opening Pandora's Box," this process keeps the participant focused and the energy contained and safe by maintaining the focus on breath, vocalizing and hitting the pillow.*

9. If someone is in a wheelchair, put the pillow on a chair in front of him/her at the same level as the wheelchair seat. If individuals do not have use of their arms, stand behind them and move their arms for them, hitting the pillow as they breathe in and vocalize. Or use your own arms or ask another student to hit the pillow for them as they breathe and vocalize.

> *On one occasion I was a quadriplegic client's arms hitting the pillow as he breathed in and expressed "no" and whatever else he needed to say when he yelled out, "Harder, hit the pillow harder for me!"*

10. Leader says, "Now please close your eyes. Imagine, or see in your mind, a person who loves you. Feel their love. Take in a deep breath and feel that love in your heart. Breathe out. Good. Breathe in again. Feel that love in your chest. Breathe out. Good. Breathe in again. Feel how thankful you are for the love. Let that feeling of thankfulness and love fill your whole body as you let out your breath. Good."

11. Leader says, "When you're ready, please open your eyes and look at the people in the room. Look into their eyes. See how they care about you. If you feel like it, you may say 'thank you' to the group."

Be sure to tell parents that you are teaching this method to their children. It's a good technique to use in the privacy of one's own room (with the windows closed) to get out frustrations. But it can be frightening to parents if they don't know what their son or daughter is up to.

Activity: Coloring
Follow these steps:
1. Leader introduces the activity saying that this is another Yes-No Process activity and that everyone will be coloring.
2. Leader holds up some crayons to the group. Leader says that each person is to come up and choose a color that seems to say "no" to him or her.
3. Each student, individually, comes up to choose a color that says "no." Each student says, "I want the (whatever) color," as each chooses a crayon.
4. When everyone has their crayon, leader instructs the class to draw a picture with their "no" crayon that says "no". Leader explains this by saying that if the students were unable to talk and needed to draw a picture to say "no," this picture will say "no" for them.
5. Everyone draws a "no" picture.
6. Leader instructs each person to stand up, show the picture drawn, and say, "No!"
7. Individually, each student stands up, shows his or her picture, and says, "No!"
8. After each person has shown their picture to the group, do the same sequence using a color that seems to say "yes." Continue with a "maybe" or "I'll think about it" color and drawing. Activity can also be adapted to:
    a. feelings (happy, angry and sad colored drawing).
    b. body (dance) and facial movements expressing "No," "Yes" and "Maybe;" or other feelings.
    c. playing musical instruments that can be made by the students. Example, a drum or tambourine could express "No" and "Yes" and different feelings depending on how it's played.

Activity: Saying "No"
   Maturity level: age 4+
The following are specific objectives for learning:
1. To promote confidence and skill in decision making.
2. To learn how to say "no" and still be liked.
3. To experience group support for expressing and hearing "yes" and "no" and accepting "yes" and "no" graciously.
4. To become aware when saying "no" and communicating "yes" and vice versa (mixed messages).
5. To become aware of body language contradicting the verbal message "yes" or "no".
6. To alleviate parental fear of a son or daughter being victimized.
7. To learn appropriate hugging habits.
8. To awaken clients to the possibilities and dangers involved in going off with a stranger.
9. To learn the difference between sexual and nonsexual touching.
10. To learn the difference between appropriate and inappropriate touching with a stranger and that with a friend, relative and authority figure.

A belief that keeps us insecure and fearful is: If I say "no" to someone, I will lose that person as my friend, I will lose love, I will lose approval.

The reality is: When you communicate clearly you say what you mean. You do not lose a real friend when you say what you mean. The more you can feel free to say "no," the more free and truthful you are when you say "yes."

The easier this becomes for you, the more honest you are with yourself and others. You might find yourself having fewer superficial friends but you'll notice how the friendship with your real friends will be so much deeper and satisfying.

So many times we end up compromising ourselves because we think that we really cannot say "no." There are times when we may want physical closeness and intimacy with a special friend without any sexual exchange but we think that if we say "no" to sexual intercourse we won't get the closeness either.

You can communicate clearly and say: "Well, I'm not ready for that but I'm ready for you holding me and for me holding you and just feeling close." You don't have to compromise yourself. Just be clear in your communication. Say "no" if you mean "no," and say what you do want.

> **If you're not ready to decide "yes" or "no", a self-empowering option is to say: "Maybe", "I'll think about it," or "I'll get back to you later."**

TEACHING HOW TO TAKE "NO" FOR AN ANSWER
Now that we know how to say "no" and hear others say "no," we have to learn how to accept the decision when someone says "no" to us without taking it personally, without our feelings being hurt.

How can you accept "no" for an answer gracefully?

Suggested exercises to role-play:
Practice saying "no" graciously, without a mixed message.
Practice accepting "no" graciously.
Brainstorm roles for role-play situations and explore the feelings you have when someone says "no" to you.

Examples:
1. Asking someone to lend you money/use of their cell phone/etc.
2. Asking a friend for a ride home.
3. Asking someone out on a date.
4. Asking someone if the seat next to them is taken (if you may sit in that seat).
5. Asking someone out for coffee.
    a. How can you stay open and hear what the other person has to say?
    b. How can you say how you feel disappointed gracefully without anger?
6. Asking someone to be their girlfriend/boyfriend or to go steady.
    a. How can you stay open and hear what the other person has to say?
    b. How can you say how you feel disappointed gracefully without anger?
7. Trying to kiss someone who doesn't want to be kissed.
8. Calling someone on the phone to talk, but they can't talk at this time.
9. Offering someone a piece of gum, candy, etc.
10. Asking for or offering someone help or advice.

Discuss that if someone hears a "no" answer to a question such as: "Do you want to have coffee with me?," it might mean that the other person doesn't want to have coffee right now but might like to have coffee at a later date. Likewise if someone hears a "no" answer to their question: "Do you want to go steady / to be my girlfriend?," it doesn't necessarily mean that they might not want to be your friend, just not your "girlfriend" with all that it entails.

Activity: Mixed Messages
1. "How many of you have said 'yes' when you meant 'no'?" Leader explains: "We've all been in situations when we've said 'yes' when we meant 'no' and said 'no' when

we meant 'yes.'" For example, did you ever say 'yes' to someone and inside it didn't really feel true or right? Maybe you were afraid, or you didn't want to hurt someone else's feelings. Sometimes people say 'yes' when they mean 'no' because they're afraid of making someone angry, or losing their friendship or love."

2. "We're going to practice saying 'yes' and 'no' and *really mean it.*"
3. "Let's all nod our heads, 'yes,' like this."
4. The group follows the leader, motioning "yes" with their heads.
5. "Now let's say 'yes' while we also nod our heads saying 'yes.'"
6. Group follows the leader, motioning and saying "yes."
7. "Let's do the same thing with 'no.' Let's shake our heads 'no' and say 'no,' like this... Leader demonstrates.
8. Group follows leader, motioning and saying "no."
9. Leader explains mixed messages. "Sometimes we send what's called a 'mixed message.' We say 'yes' with our bodies and 'no' with our mouths; or we say 'no' with our bodies and 'yes' with our mouths." Demonstrate this by smiling and saying "no." Then say "yes" angrily - shaking the head one way but verbalizing the opposite. "These are mixed messages and they confuse people. People don't know what you mean when your face and your eyes say "yes" but your voice says "no." They get confused when your words say "yes" but your face and eyes frown indicating "no."
10. Say, "Now let's all experience giving a mixed message. Shake your heads 'yes' and meekly say 'no,' like this." Leader demonstrates. Have the group follow.
11. Say, "How did it feel doing that? How did it feel inside?"
12. Demonstrate a "yes" that clearly indicates you mean *yes.*
13. Each person takes a turn saying "yes" as if they really mean it.
14. Reinforce that emphatic "yes" with "Good!" and continue until all have had a chance.
15. Briefly discuss the process. Say "How did it feel, saying 'yes' like that? It feels good to say 'yes' like we really mean it."
16. Say. "Now, we're going to say 'no' as if we really mean it, like this." Leader demonstrates.
17. Do a "no" sequence following the preceding steps (numbers 12 through 15), substituting "no" for "yes."
18. Conclude the activity. Say, "Now you know what it feels like to say 'yes' and 'no' and really mean it. Next time you say 'yes,' **mean it**. Next time you say 'no,' **mean it**."
19. Using music if possible, lead a circle movement such as shaking or bouncing to release any remaining tensions or negative feelings.

Activity: Do You Mean "Yes"? Do You Mean "No"?
1. Form a circle.
2. Leader presents a brief discussion, reviewing saying "yes" or "no" as if we really mean it and using clear communication and body language.
3. As a group, all say "no" together, really meaning it.
4. Leader goes to the center of the circle and says "no" strongly gesturing "no" with the entire body. Leader gives a mixed message by saying "no" while smiling and touching someone seductively.
5. Ask, "Do I sound and look as if I mean it? Why? Why not?"
6. Leader asks someone else to go to the center of the circle and say "no."
7. Participant goes to the center of the circle and says "no." Leader can ask questions that require a "no" answer, for example: "Give me all your money."
8. Leader asks, "Does (this person) sound and look as if they mean it?"
9. Group decides if a clear "no" was demonstrated or if there was a mixed message, for instance, smiling while saying "no." All clap and reinforce the participant.

10. Have someone else go to the center of the circle and repeat steps 7 through 9 until all have participated.
11. Repeat steps 3 through 10 with "yes."
12. End with a joyous, enthusiastic group "yes."
13. A lively variation for this activity is as follows:
    a. Form the circle.
    b. Instruct the group that when the person in the center says "yes," everyone else says "no" in response. The person in the center then says "yes" again even more emphatically, and the group responds with "no."

    c. Reverse the "yes" and the "no."
    d. Complete the activity with "yes" responded to with "yes."

Activity: Practicing Eye Contact Awareness
1. Introduce activity as an eye contact game.
2. Demonstrate with co-leader a conversation in which one person tries to make eye contact while talking, while the other person avoids eye contact.
3. Ask for volunteers to take co-leader's role in the role of wanting to make eye contact.
4. Ask how it feels to talk to someone when they look away. Did it feel like they wanted to listen?
5. Demonstrate correct eye contact with co-leader during discussion.
6. Ask for volunteers to role-play appropriate eye contact.
7. Ask students how it feels to make eye contact. Which did they like better, making eye contact or looking away?
8. Discuss when to make eye contact and with whom. What about strangers, friends, relatives, others?
9. Discuss when it is smart NOT to make eye contact?

Activity: Freeze
In the course of teaching or demonstrating activities, it will often be necessary to cause your class to suddenly stop whatever they are doing in order to hear your next instruction or explanation. Teach your class or group to expect this and to respond appropriately.

"Does everyone know what happens when moving water suddenly freezes? The water becomes solid and stops moving. We're going to make believe that we're water. When I say 'freeze,' everybody will stop whatever they are doing and stay absolutely still as if they are frozen solid like a block of ice."

"When I tell you, everybody will start speaking to one another. When I say 'freeze,' everyone will stop speaking and be absolutely silent and still. Then say, "OK, you can start speaking again." Repeat this.

"When I tell you, everybody will stand up and walk around the room in any direction." (For wheelchair students, they can wheel around the room.) "Then, when I say 'freeze,' everyone will stop moving and stay absolutely still as if they are frozen solid like a block of ice."

Instruct everyone to get up and start walking. Then after several seconds, say "freeze" loudly and clearly. Hold everyone still for a moment and then say, "OK, you can start moving again." Repeat this.

Activity: Milling, Making Eye contact
1. Review with the group how we can tell if someone really means "yes" or really means "no." What is a mixed message?

2. Get responses from group. Did they smile when they said "no" or did they nod their head in a "yes" gesture while saying "no" or did they touch the person with a "yes" gesture while saying "no?" Did their body give a different message than their words? Reinforce all responses with "Good!" or "Right!"
3. Review how someone says "no" and really means it.
4. Get responses from the group.
5. How does someone hear "no" and not get upset or feel bad?
6. Stress the importance of eye contact in giving clear, direct messages. Say, "Remember to look someone straight in the eye when you say 'yes' or 'no' or when you hear 'no'. Let it be OK to respect 'no' for an answer."
7. Demonstrate this by going up to each person in the circle and saying "no" while looking at them straight in the eye. Each recipient practices receiving the "no" graciously in different ways while staying alert for any mixed message.
8. Say, "Now everyone will get a chance to do what I just did. Mill around the room. Stop in front of someone, look at them directly in the eye and say, 'no' clearly, without being mean. The other person says 'OK' and really means it. Then move on and go up to someone else. Do this until I say *'freeze'*." (EXTRA OPTION: If someone you talk to uses a mixed message, quickly point that out and move on to the next person.)
9. After an appropriate amount of time, one minute say, "Freeze. Now switch roles. Whoever said 'no' will now be the listener and whoever heard 'no' will now say 'no'."
10. Then tell everyone to do the same activity but this time instead of saying "no," say "No thank you."
11. Next say, "Now we'll do the same thing and say 'yes.' Go directly up to someone, look that person in the eyes, smile, and say 'yes.' Then move on to someone else. Keep doing this until I say *'freeze'*."
12. Group mills about saying "yes," making eye contact.
13. Next, make eye contact and say "thank you."
14. Discuss the process: "How did it feel to look someone in the eye and say 'yes'? How did it feel saying 'no'? How did it feel to say or hear "no thank you"? Did it feel good? Which was easier for you, saying 'yes' or saying 'no'? How did it feel to be looked in the eye and hear a 'yes,' a 'no'? Did you like this activity?"

Note that a variation of this exercise is for the individual to say "no thank you" instead of just "no." Then the response can be something like, "OK, we can still be friends." The statement is still clear, there is no mixed message, eye contact is maintained and the listener is learning how to take "no" for an answer.

"NO" AND "YES" IN THE CONTEXT OF SOCIAL RELATIONSHIPS.

Activity: Eye Contact Reinforcement to Music
1. Introduce activity as an eye contact game.
2. Instruct either males or females to go inside the circle (whichever group has fewer members).
3. Tell inside group to face outer circle and to hold hands. Instruct outer group to face inner group and to hold hands.
4. Direct the two circles to move in opposite directions when music starts and make eye contact with people they pass. Smiling is good too.
5. Say and demonstrate with co-leader, "When the music stops, everyone stop moving and drop your hands. Go up to the person in front of you, say hello, make eye contact and smile."
6. Start and stop music several times.

7. Instruct any extra person who knows how to give eye contact to be in charge of starting and stopping the music after you have role-modeled the procedure.

Activity: Introducing Friends to Each Other
1. Introduce activity by asking, "Who has friends?" If someone says they have no friends, ask group, "Are any of you his/her friend?"
2. Explain that this activity is to learn how to introduce friends to each other.
3. Explain that since we are adults, it is important to learn how to meet other adults.
4. Role model with student co-leader how to:
    a. shake hands firmly (not too hard, not too spongy).
    b. make eye contact.
    c. smile.
    d. use appropriate words of response ("pleased to meet you," etc.).
5. Form a circle and demonstrate hand-shake and eye contact. Repeat related concepts like smiling and reinforce correct responses.
6. Say: "Each of you will introduce the person standing next to you to the person standing on your other side."
7. Role model: Turn to person on your left and say: "Hi, this is my friend, ____ (person's name), and (turning to right) this is my friend ____ (other person's name)."
8. Watch as students shake hands, make eye contact and say "Nice to meet you" or something equivalent.
9. Have person on your left repeat #7 and #8.
10. Repeat until everyone has introduced and been introduced.
11. Ask, "Have you learned how to introduce your friends?"
12. Review eye contact, hand-shake, smiling and other introductory words as appropriate ways to meet new people. For more verbally advanced groups practice introducing conversations that include more information. For example: "He is from San Francisco," or "She is a really good cook," or "He really likes cats."
13. Discuss appropriate greetings for people you already know (family, peers, authority figures such as teachers or supervisors, employers). Point out that handshakes with eye contact are generally best. Hugs are usually reserved for family members and close friends.

Activity: Family/Friends/Strangers
The following are specific objectives for learning:

1. To reinforce the concepts of the difference between family, friends and strangers.
2. To develop awareness of appropriate social distancing.
3. To introduce the role-play procedure.
4. To introduce the concept of sexual harassment or unwanted sexual advances.
5. To develop an awareness of common sexual "come-on's."
6. To develop and teach behaviors for refusing a stranger's sexual advances.
7. To develop an understanding of the dangers of associating with strangers.
8. To increase the ability to say "no" in appropriate circumstances.
9. To reinforce concepts of public and private body parts and places.
10. To introduce concept of whom you can go to for help.

Note: Most sexual exploitation is not by strangers but is by family, including extended family who live in or visit victim's home, as well as assisted living providers.

Materials: Butcher paper, photos of staff, teachers, students, participant's families, paraprofessionals that the group members know, administration, principal, celebrities, school or facility nurse.

1. Hold up photos of students/clients attending the school or facility, their family (house) members, the principal/administrator, other teachers, etc., and ask students/clients if they know these people. Review members of family/household, parents, siblings, uncles, aunts or members of extended family, including assisted living providers.
2. Discuss difference between friends and acquaintances.
    a. A friend is someone you know and like; who knows you and likes you.
    b. An acquaintance is someone you have met but you don't know much about them and they don't know much about you.
3. Show photos of celebrities and ask if they know these people. Point out that if a student has never met or spoken with the celebrity, then they are not acquaintances or friends; they are still strangers.
4. State that a stranger is "someone you don't know."
5. Place butcher paper on wall, write and say: "FAMILY, FRIENDS, ACQUAINTANCES, STRANGERS," across the top of the page and draw a line underneath each word.
6. Write the client's name at the top (start with your own chart to role-play the process). Write the name of the person in the picture in the first column and where they are seen in the second column. Then ask if that person is a family member, a friend, an acquaintance or a stranger and write that in the third column.

    Ex: The chart might look like this:

Student/Client: **Martha Jones**		
NAME OF PERSON IN PICTURE	PLACE USUALLY SEEN	RELATIONSHIP: FAMILY, FRIEND, ACQUAINTANCE OR STRANGER
Carol Jones	at home	family
Michael Jackson	MTV	stranger
Jimmy Johnson	in school	friend
Uncle John	at Grandma's house	family
Alice Jackson	swimming pool	friend
Mr. Green	grocery store (owner)	acquaintance

7. Repeat process with each student. Each student may have his/her own chart.
8. Read list back to class, saying "Someone in John's family is (name)_____, who is his (father, mother, etc.). One of John's friends is (name) _____, and he sees him her at (place) _____. John met a new person, whose name is _____, at (place)_____.
9. Ask students whom they can talk to about different common topics such as sports, music, etc. Go through family, friends and strangers section of chart with selected students.
10. Gradually include topics considered private. To whom can you go for help? If you felt sick? If someone hurt your feelings? If someone kicked you or hurt you? If someone stole something from you? If someone was hurting someone you were with? If someone touched your private parts or asked you to touch their private parts? If you or someone you know got pregnant? If someone made you do something you didn't really want to do and asked you to keep it a secret… or else…?

11. You will also need to explain about authority figures who are not exactly "friends" or "acquaintances" but are not necessarily "strangers." This includes policemen, firemen, doctors, nurses, priests (ministers, rabbis), teachers, school counselors, etc. These are people who our students and clients can go to for help. Except for doctors and nurses when seen in the hospital or medical office, these people are not allowed to break the rule about touching private parts, and even doctors and nurses must ask permission first.

Activity: Role-Play Procedure, Awareness of Appropriate/Inappropriate Social Situations

Practice the freeze procedure in advance by asking group members to move freely around the room and then to stop when the leader calls out, "freeze!" as if they were a statue.

1. Leader asks students what are some appropriate ways to respond to or handle particular situations. Ex: You can't find your pen and you see someone else using your pen. Write their answers on the board.
2. Leader chooses one of the student's responses to be acted out in a role-play.
3. Set up stage area and audience area (choose a student to direct the other students where to be seated).
4. Leader describes the social situation and each step of the appropriate behavior that will be demonstrated to the class.
5. Everyone says: "Lights, camera, action!" to begin role-play.
6. Leader role-plays with co-leader the appropriate behavior.
7. Unconditional appreciation (applause) at conclusion.
8. Leader asks students questions that describe each step of the role-play. Ex: "What did you do/say to the person who was using your pen? What did (name) do in response? Then what happened?"
9. Leader chooses a student or client who volunteers to participate in the role-play with the co-leader.
10. Repeat steps 4-8
11. Note: Use "freeze" at any time to gain the attention of the group.

> Invite a group member to co-lead whenever possible.

Activity: Awareness of Comfortable/Appropriate Social Distancing
1. Review:
    a. the difference between family, friends and strangers.
    b. examples of friends and relatives.
    c. eye contact.
    d. clean breath and general grooming.
    e. any specific concerns for this group.
2. Ask students:
    a. Has anyone stood too close to you while they were talking to you? How did you feel?
    b. Have you ever stood too close to someone else while you were talking to them? How do you think they felt?
3. Demonstrate with co-leader:
    a. Standing too close to co-leader while speaking to him/her. Ask students, "Is this appropriate? - Why not?"

b. Standing across the room from the co-leader while speaking to him/her. Ask students, "Is this distance appropriate? - Why not?"
  c. Standing at about arm's length from co-leader. Ask, "Is this distance appropriate? - Why?"
  d. Raising your arm to touch the shoulder of the co-leader. Point out that you are about an arm's length from him/her and that this is the correct distance to stand next to another person.
  e. Stand several feet from co-leader. Then walk towards him/her. Ask co-leader to tell you to stop when you have reached a comfortable distance for a conversation.
  f. If co-leader/partner stands too close, practice stepping back until you are at a comfortable distance.
4. Tell students to stand and choose partners for this activity. Ask students to do activities 3 c, d, e and f (note that we do not have the students demonstrate or act out inappropriate behaviors as in a and b, except to step back if they are too close as in f).
5. Leaders or other students who are competent in this activity step up to other students and confirm that they know how to stand at **arm's length**. This is a good time to reinforce **eye contact.**
6. Point out that comfortable social distance may be different for different people. Some people may be most comfortable standing at slightly more or less than arm's length.
7. Ask each student to choose someone in the group to say "hello" to and to check for social distance at the same time.
8. Point out that they do NOT put their arms out to check this distance in public. That's just for this exercise in this class.
9. Ask students what they can do if someone is standing too close to them. Ex: step farther away.

Activity: Role-Play Eye Contact and Facial Expressions
Have the group role-play different ways of making contact and communicating different messages (for example: "yes, no." "I can't, I can." "I won't, I will." "I like you, I don't like you") through eye contact and facial expressions.

Activity: Role-Play Saying "No" to a Stranger and to People You Know
It is recommended that the leader prepare the group for this activity by warming up with some brief activity from the basic Yes-No Process.

1. Leader introduces the activity by leading a discussion on sexual harassment. One approach is to solicit descriptions of actual past experiences from group members. Another is to pose hypothetical situations.
    a. "Has a stranger ever come up to you and asked you to go for a drive?"
    b. "What if a stranger on the street tried to get you to go into a car with him?"
    c. "Has a stranger ever come up to you in a bathroom and tried to touch your private parts?" Or, "What if a stranger came up to you and tried to touch your private parts?"
    d. "What if a stranger came up to you and started to show his private parts to you?"
    e. "What if you were on a bus and someone sat next to you and started putting their arm around you or started touching you?"
2. Leader facilitates discussion with the group using brainstorm techniques:

    a. "What are some things you can do if someone tries to touch you but you don't want to be touched?"
    b. "What can you do to get away from a stranger who is bothering you?"
    c. "What can you do to get away from someone you know who is bothering you?"
3. Leader stresses the point that if a stranger approaches a student, the most important thing to do is to say "no" loudly and clearly and **walk away**.
4. Leader and co-leader demonstrate step 3 by role-playing. Leader approaches the co-leader and invites him or her to go for a drive or offers to give or show the co-leader something special. Co-leader responds by saying "no" and walking away.
5. Leader reviews the role-play with the class. "What did the stranger do? What did the co-leader do? What should you do in the same situation?"
6. Discuss what could happen to you if you went with the stranger.
7. Leader and co-leader do another role-play to exemplify what could happen if someone fails to say "no" assertively to a stranger and walk away. Leader repeats the previously demonstrated approach to co-leader; this time the co-leader fails to respond appropriately and merely stands in place. Leader's advances become increasingly aggressive until co-leader is bodily dragged away.
8. Leader discusses this second role-play with the group: "What happened that time? What did I do? What did the co-leader do? What do you think happened to the co-leader after being dragged away? Why is it so important to walk away from strangers before they can grab you?"
9. Leader and co-leader again role-play steps 3 through 5, the correct way to reject a stranger's advances.
10. Leader asks someone in the class to come up and perform a role-play. Leader again plays the part of a stranger; the student plays the part of the "victim."
11. Leader discusses the role-play with the group. If the student responded appropriately in the role-play, discuss what was done correctly and then the group gives their applause. If the student responded inappropriately, discuss the consequences of that action and what could have been done differently. Repeat the role-play again. Keep repeating until the student succeeds.
12. Role-plays continue in the manner just described until all participants have performed. Possible variations are having two students participate in the role-play or having students devise new scenarios, still along the theme of sexual harassment.

On one of our field trips to a museum we brought along our portable video unit to test our students in real life situations. We had previously gone through numerous role-playing activities. We asked a friend at the museum to approach several female students individually and ask them to go for a ride in his car. The first girl he approached said "no" appropriately and walked away. The second one thought about it for a moment but then accepted going off with the stranger. The third girl accepted right away. We learned that those last two students were not ready to go out on their own and we shared that experience with their parents. Later, back in the classroom, we found it valuable to have the videotapes of that encounter to show to the students. Peer pressure was strongly against their decisions to go off with the strangers, but to see if they learned and were ready to be unsupervised in public we would need to set up another new situation with these students to see if they would go off with a stranger again.

13. If a stranger grabs a person's wrists, remember that the thumbs are the most vulnerable part. Pull your wrists away from the stranger's grasp in the direction of the stranger's thumbs. You will need to demonstrate this. Give each student a

chance to grab another person's wrists and watch how their grip is released when the other person breaks away from the encircling thumbs. After breaking away, change roles.

It is not within the scope of this program to teach self-defense techniques. But we are attempting to create the attitudes of correct defense. Depending on the sophistication of your group, it may be appropriate to invite a self-defense teacher (perhaps someone from the local police department or a martial arts group) to speak or demonstrate to your group.

14. Depending on the age and sophistication of your group, you may want to add this: "Sometime, perhaps when you are older, you may want to be touched or to touch the private parts of someone else, or that person may want to touch your private parts. You might be engaged or married to that person. You both consent to being sexually intimate together privately. If you are in a private place and you both want to be sexual then it can be OK. If you are both ready for the responsibility of sexual intimacy including birth control and the prevention of sexually transmitted disease you need permission only from each other."

Activity: Balloons (adapted from Daniel Malamud, Ph.D.)
   Maturity level: age 5+
Specific objective for learning: To review, evaluate and improve the ability to say "no" to requests.
1. Leader introduces the activity, saying that everyone will have a chance to choose a balloon, blow it up and play with it.
2. Leader gives the instructions that students will come up one-at-a-time to get a balloon. Each can pick the color balloon wanted and must ask for it by using a complete sentence (e.g., "I want a [red] balloon"). Each person will say "thank you" after receiving a balloon and receive unconditional appreciation from the group.
3. Each student, in turn, chooses a balloon.
4. All blow up their balloons. Leader or other person assists those who have difficulty blowing up a balloon <u>after they ask for help</u>.
5. All play with their balloons, bouncing them into the air to background music.
6. Each person gives their balloon a name. Share the name with the group. Individuals tell how they feel playing with their balloons. Ex: "My balloon's name is 'Sunny' and I feel happy playing with Sunny."
7. Leader tells everyone to break their balloons.
8. All break balloons.
9. If anyone refuses to break their balloon, tell them that you will respect their decision and they need not break their balloon because you can take "no" for an answer.
10. Leader discusses the activity: "How did it feel to break the balloon? Did you want to break the balloon? Have you ever had to do something you did not want to do? If so, when? What happened?"
11. Option: At a later date repeat this exercise giving group the opportunity to make a different choice, to say "no" assertively when being told to break their balloons.
12. Role-play situations where requests or demands should be assertively and vigorously rejected:
    a. Someone demanding money or other possession.
    b. Someone pressuring you to do something that you don't want to do.
    c. Someone demanding that the student pulls down his or her pants.

Activity: Forced Choice "Think For Yourself"
   Maturity level: age 5+
1. Introduce activity as an independent decision-making "think for yourself" choosing game. That means going inside yourself and deciding what **you** think and what **you** choose. It doesn't matter what the other people here choose.
2. Ask students if they ever had to choose between two things to **have**, to **do** or to **be**. Give concrete examples. It is best to start the game with light and humorous choices.
    a. Which is your favorite ice cream? Raise your hand if you choose chocolate. Now raise your hand if you choose vanilla.
    b. How would you prefer to walk? Raise your hands if it's on your hands. Now raise your hands if it's on your feet?
    c. Would you rather be happy or sad?
    d. Laugh or cry?
    e. Go to a party or go to bed?
3. Instruct as follows:
    a. Students stand in middle of room.
    b. Leader will give two choices.
    c. Students who make first choice will go to one side of room. Students who make second choice will go to other side of room.
4. Say: "Everyone who wants to (say choice), go to this side of the room (point). Everyone who wants to (say choice), go to the other side of the room (point)."
5. Here are various choices:
    a. Everyone who is a male go to this side of the room and everyone who is a female go to that side of the room.
    b. Everyone with blue eyes go to this side of the room, brown eyes to that side of the room.
    c. Is wearing certain colors.
    d. Is wearing a dress or skirt, or is wearing slacks or pants.
    e. Prefers to be tall or short.
    f. Prefers to be a baby-sitter or a baby.
    g. Prefers to be a teacher or a student.
    h. Prefers to go off with a stranger, or say "no" and walk away (note: if any student says he/she prefers to go off with a stranger, ask that person and the group to list possible consequences of going with strangers)
    i. Choices between different job possibilities, etc.
6. Ask students to give reason(s) for their choice, co-leader goes first.
7. Ask students how they feel when they are outnumbered by their friends (i.e. they made the less popular choice).
8. Use as many choices/examples as time and attention span permits.
9. Option: Group wears blindfolds to prevent peer influence in making choices.

Discuss how we make choices every day with different people making different choices for different reasons. Review some choices in the above activity as examples of these differences. Point out that it's okay for people to make different choices, that everyone is different and that differences are normal.

   Maturity level: adolescence to adulthood.
10. When you are using this exercise during the lesson on procreation or birth control, you may use the following additional choices:
    a. People who want to have jobs vs. people who want to help at home.

b. People who are ready to make a baby and stay home to take care of the baby vs. people who want to have freedom to be able to have a good time when they want and go to parties.
   c. People who want to spend their money on taking care of a baby vs. people who want to spend their money for/on themselves.
   d. People who feel ready for sex vs. people who want to wait until they meet the right person.
   e. Discuss the choices afterward.

If someone is in a sexually responsible relationship and there is mutual consent, it may be appropriate to agree to be touched sexually. The appropriate response will depend on their readiness for this kind of activity.

Activity: Is it OK or not?
Maturity level: age 5+
During the lesson on sexual exploitation use these choices (after reviewing public and private parts). Put sign stating "OK" on one wall and "NOT OK" on the other wall.:
Go to one side of the room if it's OK or the other side if it's not OK.
   a. People who would go off with a stranger vs. people who would say "no" and walk away.
   b. People who would hitch-hike or get in a car with a stranger vs. people would take the bus.
   c. People who would let someone touch their private parts (penis, vagina, breasts, rear-end) vs. people who would say "no" and get away.
   d. People who would let a stranger on a bus touch them vs. people who would move to another seat on the bus, far away from this person.
   e. If you are asked to touch someone's private parts (even someone you know), are you someone who would agree and do it or are you someone who would say "no" and walk away? Is it OK or not OK? Move to appropriate side of room.
   f. Is it OK for anyone in your house or family to touch your private parts or is it not OK? Move to appropriate side of room.
   g. Is it OK to say "no" and get away if anyone in your house or family tries to touch your private parts or is it not OK to say "no" to them? Move to appropriate side of room.
   h. Is it OK to put your lips or your mouth on the private parts (penis, vagina, breasts, rear-end) of someone who lives with you or is it not OK? Move to appropriate side of room.
   i. Is it OK to say "no" and get away from someone who lives with you who asks you to put your lips or your mouth on their private parts or is it not OK to say "no"? Move to appropriate side of room.
   j. Is it OK to tell a secret if someone wants you to keep a secret but it doesn't feel right? Is it OK to tell or is it not OK to tell?

Discuss these choices without shaming. Talk about people you can go to for help: at home, at school, at work, at a social agency.

TO WHOM CAN YOU GO FOR HELP?

This is an important question for people at all levels of maturity whether challenged or not. Many so-called "normal" people assume that if they need help someone will simply "read their mind" and offer help but this is not so. Many individuals (including parents) have difficulty asking for help. They are not certain what to ask for, how to ask for it and whom to ask.

Specific objective: To identify a support network of professionals, specialists and reliable friends who are available to help individuals in need.

1. List people students can go to for help. Identify how each person could be helpful.
    a. Provide photos or drawings of the people or resources available.
    b. Invite these people to the class to introduce themselves and how they help people in the group.
    c. Examples include: facility nurse/doctor (health professionals), social worker(s), Rape Relief organization representative, Planned Parenthood representative, Crisis Line representative, Association for Retarded Citizens representative, policeman/woman, bus driver, etc.
2. Identify specific situations in which help would be needed. Describe each situation.
    a. You or someone else feels sick or has pain.
    b. You or someone else is extremely sick, has severe pain or was just seriously injured. There is an immediate medical emergency.
    c. You are lost and don't know how to get home.
    d. There is a fire.
    e. A stranger tries to get you into a car.
    f. A stranger bothers you while you are waiting for a bus or riding on a bus.
    g. Someone you know (perhaps in your family/home) is touching your private parts with their hands or mouth or having you do that to them.
    h. Someone you know (perhaps where you live) is having sexual activity with you. (See chapter on sexual activity)

It is important that when victims and perpetrators are identified, appropriate support systems are in place to help resolve the situations/problems.

   i. Familiarize and give each student an individualized list of names and phone numbers they can access for help. Discuss how to use 911 and telephone operator. Rehearse / role-play telephoning, asking for help and reporting relevant information.

Note to the leader: Speaking of asking for help, as a teacher/facilitator you may find that you can use some help. One cannot overestimate the power of a prayer; so we now include a nondenominational prayer that has helped many people and may help you.

> Eternal God,
> As I begin again this voyage of
> learning and teaching
> I pause for this moment
> to reaffirm my bearings.

Rekindle in me, I pray,
    the flame of learning.
Renew in me I pray,
    the excitement of teaching.
Help me to chart my course
    straight and true,
        drifting neither toward
            the shoals of cynicism
                nor the shallows of
                    mediocrity.

Restore in me, I pray,
    pride in my craft,
        confidence in my skill,
            compassion for my students,
                and a deepened sense of
                    brotherhood amongst
                        us all.

And grant me Godspeed
    in the journey before me.
    Amen.

TOUCHING AND BEING TOUCHED

From the day we were born, we all needed human contact to touch and be touched appropriately. Babies need to be held close, cuddled and touched to enable their nervous systems to develop normally and to feel loved and cared for.

Research has shown that babies in orphanages who had little physical contact or holding or touch, their bottles propped up during feeding, did not receive the stimulation needed to develop a normal nervous system. A number of these individuals grew up emotionally unstable and became social outcasts (criminals). Even as adults we all need daily physical contact that feels good. We all need to be held and cared for. Dr. Leo Buscaglia says that we all need at least ten hugs to get through the day.

Many of our clients are comfortable giving and receiving hugs but they get into trouble when they hug people who are not comfortable giving or receiving hugs or mistake the innocence of a hug for a sexual opportunity. To protect our clients and students until society is ready for their innocent embraces, we have to teach them to hold back their hugs and shake hands instead. Wouldn't this be a wonderful planet if its people were trustworthy and comfortable giving and receiving hugs to each other without discrimination and fear? In the meantime, we teach how to shake someone's hand and be aware of those people who may not even feel comfortable giving a handshake. We remind our students that people have different levels of comfort when it comes to being touched; it needn't be taken personally.

Activity: Tension Release
    Maturity level: all levels.
This activity is especially helpful when people need to relax at the beginning of a group session. It's a useful precursor to the subsequent touching activities. Play soft background music.
1. Form a circle.
2. Everyone stand with knees slightly bent.

3. Stand tall with good posture.
4. Everyone, together, breathe in through your nose, and out through your mouth, five times.
5. Say: "We're going to shake out tension and tightness in our bodies."
6. Gently shake your
    a. hands.
    b. arms.
    c. shoulders.
        (1. up and down.
        (2. roll forward.
        (3. roll backward.
    d. hips.
    e. knees.
    f. right foot.
    g. left foot.
7. Tilt your head slowly to the right and to the left, up and down.
8. Do the Hokey-Pokey.

Activity: Handshaking Practice
Maturity level: all levels.
Before starting, ask everyone if their hands are clean. If not, ask them to wash.
1. Take turns shaking each other's hand with eyes closed.
2. Take turns shaking each other's hand with eyes open, making eye contact.
3. Discuss and try out different handshakes. Handshakes tell you something about the person. What do these handshakes tell you?
    a. A loose grip like a wet sponge.
    b. Completely passive.
    c. With just a few fingers.
    d. Squeezing too hard.
    e. A firm handshake.
4. Discuss which kind of handshake:
    a. felt good?
    b. did not feel good?
    c. How did you experience yourself?
    d. How did you experience your partner?
5. Practice a firm handshake while making eye contact and smiling.

Activity: Circle Massage
Maturity level: all
Before starting, ask if everyone's hands are clean. If not, ask them to wash.
   Everyone including the leader and co-leader stand or sit in a circle. All turn to the right so that each person faces the back of the person to their right.
   Role model each of the following steps:
1. Ask the person in front of you for their permission to massage their shoulders and back.
2. Gently place your hands on the shoulders of the person in front of you.
3. Demonstrate and describe as you role model squeezing the shoulders of the person in front of you gently.
4. Ask person if it feels OK. "Is it too strong a squeeze or too weak?" If they would like a stronger squeeze wait for feed-back. Ex: "Does that feel OK? Would you like me to squeeze softer, harder?"

5. Invite group to do activity.
6. Ask everyone to turn to the other direction (the left) for exchange of massages.
7. When finished, ask group how it felt. "What did you like? What didn't you like?"
8. Variations:
    a. Demonstrate light-touch exercises on the back, shoulders and arms such as tapping or gentle chopping with the side of the hands.
    b. Then invite group to do the exercise.
    c. Then share experiences using the preceding questions.
9. Explore and get acquainted with another's hands with eyes closed, and progress to wrists, forearms, elbows and upper arms. Do activity in pairs.
    a. Try different squeezes and pressures.
    b. Holding hands, allow your hands to express how they feel about your partner's hands, to your partner's hands.
    c. Discuss these feelings.
10. Let everyone in the group put their hands in a pile with eyes closed; the bottom hand lifts to the top.

Activity: Palm Conversation Dance
1. Pairs of students face each other and place their hands against each other's hands. Eyes are closed. Students do this exercise without speaking. (Note: For those students requiring more body support, this exercise can be done with two wheelchairs facing each other. If students' handicap prohibits hand motion, use heads [face or forehead] or any parts of the body that do move.) Explain:
2. Introduce your hands to your partner's hands.
3. Let your hands get to know each other. Use your fingers, palms, hands.
4. Have a conversation-dance with your hands.
5. Have a palm-dance pretending you're having a disagreement, an argument or rejection.
6. Gradually make up and be gentle.
7. Do a happy, fun palm-dance.
8. Dance as though your hands are in love; allow the dance to flourish into sweeping movements.

Activity: Class Handshake Review:
A good activity to start a class, a way to say hello.
1. Review firm hand shake, eye contact, smiling, good posture.
2. Everyone mingles around the room shaking hands.
3. How did each of you experience yourself? Each other? How did you feel?

Activity: Preventing Victimization and Sexual Exploitation
   Maturity level: age 5+
Touching to express affection:
   While giving and receiving affection are some of the primary ingredients for feeling good about yourself and others, the expression of affection in some situations is not always considered socially acceptable. It is useful to know about the social implications of affectionate touch.
1. Review concepts of family, friends and strangers.
2. Ask: "When do we touch people in public?"
    a. Greeting people? Whom do you greet?
    b. Going through a crowd? How do you touch?
    c. Getting someone's attention? How?
    d. Dancing? Who? How? When? Where?

e. Congratulating someone? How? Whom?
   f. First aid? Whom do you ask for help? How?
   g. Kissing? Whom? How? When? Where?
      (1. Quickly, in greeting.
      (2. Slowly, long time.
      (3. French kissing.
      (4. Kissing on forehead, cheek, lips, neck, hand.
   h. Hugging? Who?
      (1. Quickly, in greeting.
      (2. Slowly, long time.
      (3. Close, full body hug.
   i. Holding hands? With whom?
   j. Touching genitalia.
      (1. Review concepts of public and private places and body parts.
      (2. Indicate that genitalia were never touched during the circle massage activity.
      (3. Ask: "Would it be OK to touch genitalia in the classroom or at work?"
      (4. Is it OK for a teacher to touch your private parts (your penis, your vagina, your breasts, your buttocks, your thighs)?
      (5. Is it OK for a doctor to touch your private parts?
      (6. Is it OK for your sister, brother, uncle, aunt, father or mother, to touch your private parts? Is it OK to touch their private parts?
      (7. If you meet a stranger, is it OK for the stranger to touch your private parts?
      (8. If you meet a stranger, is it OK to touch the stranger's private parts?
      (9. Is it OK for your care provider (say name) to touch your private parts?
      (10. Is it OK for a priest or minister to touch your private parts or ask you to touch his/her private parts?
3. State: "If anyone tries to touch your private parts tell them, 'No!' and walk away." Use drawings of authority figures.
4. Ask: "If you try to touch someone and they say 'No,' do you have to stop? What can happen to you if you keep touching them?"

Here is a true story about a young man, a Special Ed student named Tom who was doing well in life. He was becoming a man, he felt good about himself, but his social skills were lacking. He had a job, he knew how to use public transportation, but no one ever explained to him that he could get into trouble if he touched someone inappropriately. One day Tom was riding the bus to the sheltered workshop where he worked. He saw a pretty ten-year-old girl on the bus and he wanted to become friends with her. She appeared to be alone on the bus. He got out of his seat and touched her to get her attention. He wanted to have a conversation with her because he was lonely. She was frightened and ignored him but he kept trying to get her attention by touching her. He touched her on her shoulder, he touched her on her head, he didn't know he was being inappropriate. The bus driver noticed what was happening in his rear view mirror. He also could hear this young man speaking to this little girl. The bus driver, who also happened to be the little girl's father, thought that his daughter was in danger. He stopped the bus and had Tom arrested.

His teacher visited Tom in prison. She was so upset with the way that Tom looked. They shaved his head and he was wearing prison clothing. He was miserable.

"Nobody ever told me that I could get into trouble and be put in jail if I tried to make friends with a little girl and I touched her. I didn't know it was wrong. Now I'm in BIG trouble." He broke down and cried, *"I want to get out of here!"*

The little girl didn't even say "no" to Tom but he was still arrested for inappropriate touching. It's called sexual harassment.

5. State that victimization can happen to males as well as to females. Everyone needs to be careful. Brainstorm how Tom could have avoided getting into trouble and not been arrested.
6. Optional: You may use butcher paper to write down (brainstorm) appropriate and inappropriate touching behaviors. Include: doctors, police, firefighters, landlords, relatives, friends, strangers, married couples, priests, etc.

DEVELOPING SOCIALIZATION SKILLS

An important part of feeling like other people is to feel connected to others socially. Life can feel empty without friends. We all need to learn how to appropriately make and keep friends.

The following are specific objectives for learning social skills:
1. Identify and reinforce individuals' strengths in a (group) social context.
2. Practice asking for help during group activity.
3. Reinforce eye contact awareness in social situations.
4. Review how to introduce yourself with a firm handshake.
5. Rehearse how to introduce our friends to each other.
6. Review and rehearse a comfortable social distance.
7. Introduce and rehearse communicating necessary information and making plans to get together.
8. Review good grooming habits.
9. Review difference between family, friends, acquaintances and strangers.
10. Develop leadership skills by co-leading role-modeling activities.

The people we work with often have had limited appropriate socialization experiences and/or opportunities to succeed socially. They need to rehearse developmentally to learn their socialization skills. Many daily socialization skills that we take for granted have to be taught developmentally, deliberately and creatively and patiently repeated.

These self-esteem principles bear repetition. They will guide you toward success.

SELF-ESTEEM PRINCIPLE #1:
Each of us is individual and unique, and we are also like other people.

SELF-ESTEEM PRINCIPLE #2:
The ongoing success of the participant is more important than predetermined goals, objectives or expectations.

Activity: The Guessing Card Game: "Who Am I?"
   Maturity level: age 7+
Review each participant's strengths you have charted before beginning this activity. See section on Strength Assessment, page 21. Choose one or more strengths as "clues."

Write these "clues" about each participant on a separate piece of paper or 3" x 5" card.
1. Introduce activity as a guessing game.
2. Say, "I have these cards/this paper. Each card has clues, words describing one of you. We are going to guess whom the card is about. If the card is about you, keep it a secret for now."
3. "Everyone will pick one of these cards. When it is your turn you can read the card or you can ask for help reading it."
4. "Who wants to pick the first card?"
5. Read the clues. Remind group, "If the card is about you, keep it a secret."
6. The group guesses the person's identity.

7. When person is guessed, ask "Is this you?"
8. Have person repeat after you the points or descriptions in the clue (for example: "I am a female with clean, long brown hair. I like to help Theresa comb and style her hair").
9. Repeat numbers 4, 5, 6, 7 and 8. Note: If person's identity is not guessed, continue to give more clues until someone guesses the correct identity.

Activity: Effective Communication Techniques Practice
See page 13: Reinforcement Techniques for Developing Self-Esteem

Review and role model importance of
1. making eye contact.
2. referring to person by name.
3. smiling, listening.
4. responding to person.
5. paraphrasing, repeating back what they heard.
6. answering questions enthusiastically.

Prepare some topics to use for discussion in advance (ex: What did you do yesterday? How are you feeling today?). Use the Feeling Good Question Cards (see Resources) or Strength Assessment Questions (page 21). Ask participants to choose a partner to practice communication skills.

RELATIONSHIPS AND DATING

The following are specific objectives for learning:
1. To relate nonverbally and verbally with awareness.
2. To become aware of different ways to interpret someone's friendliness.
3. To become aware of how/when students relate to others on an emotional level.
4. To become aware of characteristics important in choosing a date.
5. To become aware of characteristics unimportant in choosing a date.
6. To become aware of personal expressions of masculinity and femininity.
7. To become aware of how we automatically classify information into sex roles.
8. To become aware of how we know when we're in love or not in love.
9. To become aware of how the advertising media reinforce role images and behavior.

10. To discuss different aspects and interpretations of "making out."
11. To express fears, excitement, expectations of making out, petting and "going steady."
12. To inform students about homosexual and bisexual behavior and myths without bias.
13. To share feelings and attitudes about homosexuality.

NONVERBAL AND VERBAL COMMUNICATION

Activity: Discussion About Touching:
Maturity level: age 12+
Each person has his or her own touch and own experience in touching and being touched.
1. In what ways were you touched by your parents when you were a child?
2. Is touching to express anger acceptable at your home? What about punishment? (Hitting, spanking, other physical measures?)
3. Is touching to express affection acceptable at your home?
4. How do your parents express affection for each other nonverbally? Toward your siblings? Toward you?
5. How do you express your affection to relatives, friends, etc.?

Activity: Back Talk
A nonverbal back-to-back conversation. This is done by placing two persons (standing or seated on floor) back-to-back in contact with one another. No talking is allowed. Eyes may be closed. The leader then suggests different "conversations" as follows. Add your own variations. *(Note: you may want to clear the area and put mats on the floor for students to sit on.)*
1. Introduce your back to your partner's back.
2. Move your back against your partner's back so as to get to know each other.
3. Have a back argument.
4. Make up, be gentle.
5. Be playful.
6. Thank your partner.
7. Slowly separate backs, experience your back, open eyes, and see your partner.
8. Students share (verbally) with their partner or the group how they felt doing the exercise.

Activity: A Love Letter
It's a good practice to regularly take time out for yourself to reflect, to re-evaluate your priorities, to consider who or what activities give you energy, what and who take too much of your energy with too little reward, and consider changes you are ready to make. This may also be a time to count your blessings and appreciate yourself, to take note of how far you have come in your life. This is useful for the teacher's own well being as well as an activity for the teacher to offer to the class.

Write a love letter to yourself, address it to yourself and mail it to yourself.

TURNING OURSELVES ON AND OFF TO OTHERS

Activity: Discussion
Maturity level: age 13+
What are the things that attract you to girls/women? To boys/men?
1. What do you do if you have an erection in public?

2. What do you do if you feel wet between your legs?
   a. Is it okay?
   b. Is it normal?
3. What turns you off to girls/women? To boys/men? What bugs you about the opposite sex? Your own sex? What can you do or say if someone is too aggressive? Role-play different strategies.
4. What is a "date"?
5. Who is a date?
6. How do you ask someone for a date? What needs to be communicated? Role-play.
   a. The activity (a movie, dinner, coffee, a party).
   b. The place.
   c. The day, date and time.
   d. Transportation.
   e. Cost of the date – who pays for what? What are ways to remember to bring money? What are the consequences of forgetting to bring money?
7. How do you say "I like you" in different ways? (Role-play verbally and nonsexually: facial expressions, gestures, body language, etc.)
8. Describe the "perfect" partner. Talk about categories that may include:
   a. Appearance – Do they have good grooming? How they look to you?
   b. Personality – What does this mean to you? Look up the meaning in the dictionary.
   c. Intelligence – What do they know? What do they talk about? What do they care about?
   d. Social class – What are examples of social class? What category are you?
   e. How does that other person make you feel about them and yourself?
   Note: Ask participants to reflect on their own appearance, personality, desirability, and how they can improve (perhaps use a full-length mirror), etc.
9. What are the characteristics in this "perfect" partner that you see in yourself?
10. The "perfect" person would be just like me *except* for…

Activity: Play "The Dating Game"
Maturity level: 13+
1. Ask each participant to bring two pictures of persons of the same or opposite sex that are attractive to them (turn them on) and two that repel them (turn them off), from magazines, albums, newspapers, etc.
2. Make up and read (one at a time) descriptions of different types of people, omitting the gender, thus incorporating the awareness of sex roles and how they affect our relationships. Each participant rates how they would like to date the person described. Individual responses are essential as opposed to group consensus.

   Rating System: 1 through 5
   1 This person *really* turns me on!
   2 I would enjoy dating this person very often.
   3 I might occasionally date this person.
   4 I would not date this person.
   5 I don't want to know this person.

3. After each participant has rated the person described, each shares his or her rating.
4. Show the class a picture of the person described. (The teacher chooses from pictures that students have brought to class.) Students now give another rating with the added visual information.

5. Discussion: Use questions like "What happened to change your desire for that person?" This is an excellent time to point out how often people make judgments about each other from just looking at them. Offer a new perspective to students in understanding the non-handicapped world; how they are very much a part of that world in the way that they view people.
6. For variation, show a picture first, rate, read the description, rate again. Talk about the judgments, feelings, attitudes, images, individual needs and desires experienced.

Activity: Discussion of Intimacy
   Maturity level: age 13+
1. Kissing:
   Review different kinds of kisses (on forehead, cheek, hand, lips, neck, etc.).
   What do different kisses communicate in different situations?
2. How can you tell the difference between a friendly kiss (nonsexual) and a sexual kiss? Would a "French kiss" (when one person puts their tongue into the other person's mouth) be appropriate to give to your father? Your aunt? Your sister? A new friend? A boy or girl friend? When? Where?
3. Petting:
   What is "petting?"
   Above the waist, below the waist, outside clothing, underneath clothing.
4. How do you know when you and the other person are ready for making out or petting? Explain that "making out" is a general term referring to kissing and petting.
5. How do you ask for permission?
   Review saying "no" and accepting "no" graciously.
6. When and where would each be appropriate or inappropriate?
7. With whom?

Activity: Discussion of Going Steady
1. What does it mean to "go steady," to "be engaged?"
2. Why or why not should a person "go steady?"
3. Who decides? Who agrees? How do you reach the decision?
4. What commitments are involved?
5. Who does what when you are part of a couple? What are the expectations?

Activity: Discussion of Falling in Love
   Maturity level: age 12+
Love is not only an emotion, it is an action, how one behaves with another. Sharing thoughts and feelings about love can be enriching. Examples: Do you know anyone who fell in love but later fell out of love? What happened? What are some signs that a partner is wrong for you?
1. What is NOT love?
   Brainstorm examples to illustrate the following list:
   a. If someone has sex with you, does that mean that they love you?
      For two people to have a love together that lasts a long time, it usually takes time to develop and grow. Many people confuse sex with love. "About the dumbest thing anyone can do is to marry for sex. If sex is the only thing to look forward to in a marriage, don't marry at all. It's not worth it."*

---

* How Do You Know When You're Really In Love?" by Sol Gordon, Ph.D.
♦ "Rock-a-Bye-Baby," A Time-Life Documentary Film

Give your relationship time. There is no rush to have sex. Sex is not going to make someone love you or make love stay. It is better to take the time to become good friends and really get to know each other before having a sexual relationship. It is possible to be in love more than once in your life "The challenge is to fall in love and stay in love during all the changes that life brings."*

b. Jealousy (ex: not allowing you to have your own friends, overly possessive).
c. Lies (not telling the truth).
d. Verbal abuse (put-downs, negativity, words that hurt your feelings).
e. Physical abuse (squeezing too hard, hitting, slapping, hurting your body).
f. Meanness (being inconsiderate).
g. A romantic movie or romance novel.
h. Great body, good looks.
i. Liking the same movies.
j. Rich, buys you presents, has a nice car, nice clothes, house, apartment.
k. Gets angry or cries a lot.
l. Passion.
m. Has sex with other people, fools around.
n. Unkept promises, ex: "Don't worry honey. After we're married, I'll stop flirting."
o. Borrows your money or things, or doesn't return what they borrowed. *(Do you feel used?)*
p. Your parents or friends are telling you that you SHOULD love a certain person, a "good catch."
q. They smile at you.
r. Feeling turned on, physically, emotionally excited.
s. Being the same religion.
t. Asking repeatedly, "Do you love me, do you really love me?"
u. Intimacy.
v. A one way relationship (feelings of love are not returned).

2. "Lines" that boys give girls to get sex.
Ask your class if they have ever heard these lines before or if they (or anyone they know) ever used these lines. In the columns below, possible responses are shown as well. Brainstorm other lines and appropriate responses. These lines can easily be play-acted. Preparing girls to anticipate phony lines like these will give them some ammunition when they are challenged, even if it just gets them to laugh when someone tries to use a line.

What if he says:	Just say in response:
"If we don't do it I'll go crazy."	"Go." (No one has ever died from an unrelieved erection.)
"So many girls say 'no' when they mean 'yes'."	"When I mean 'yes,' you'll know."
"You bring out the animal in me."	"I never wanted the animal – just the person."
"Would you like to make love?"	"Out of what?"
"Let's do it. I'll be your best friend."	"I'm my own best friend."
"Sex isn't such a big deal. What are you waiting for?"	"I'm waiting for someone it's a big deal with."
"You can't leave me this way."	"Watch me."
"You wouldn't want to hurt my feelings, would you?"	"Better than my reputation."
"I have disappointment after disappointment these days, so don't put me down by saying that you won't come home with me."	"Okay, I won't say it, but I won't come home with you either."
"I just want to show you how much I love you."	"Save the show and stick to the tell."
"If you really love me, you'll show me."	"I'll show you, right to the door."
"I'll respect you in the morning."	"Good, then I'll see you tomorrow."
"Want to have oral sex?"	"Yeah, let's just talk about it."
"Say you love me. Say you love me."	"You love me."
"I don't have any luck with girls."	"Well, perhaps you should try having a conversation with one."
"You would (have sex) if you loved me."	"If you loved me you wouldn't put that kind of pressure on me."
"All the other girls do it."	"Then do it with all the other girls."

"The question to ask is not if I feel that I'm really in love, but rather, is the love I feel the kind of love on which I can build a lasting relationship or marriage." (Ira Reiss)

3. Am I really in love or infatuated?
    Dr. Gordon* suggests that we ask ourselves the following questions:
    Have I reasonably concluded that the person I love:
    a. Can be trusted?
    b. Seems to love me?
    c. Is loyal?
    d. Is a good friend?
    e. Would make a good parent if we decided to have or adopt children?
    f. Could be moody and have some problems but is basically kind and compassionate?
    g. Respects me and cares about my welfare, about what happens to me?
    h. Can handle inevitable conflicts with maturity and considered (and appropriate) action?
    i. Thinks first before he/she acts?
    j. Has control over the volatile and often destructive emotion of anger?
    k. Enjoys my company and vice versa, and we both like each other?
    l. Has a lot in common with me that we talk about.

These key questions take time to answer. *"That's why the early stages (the first six months) of being in love are so tricky."*

4. How do you know when you're in love? (Good for parents' group too!)
    a. What is love? What do you like about love? Who needs love? What do you do with love?
    b. How can you tell if you love someone? How do you feel?
    c. How can you tell if someone loves you? How do you feel? Do you have to do anything with their love?
    d. Does everyone know how to love? How do we learn how to love? (suggested film: "Rock-a-bye-Baby" about Harlow's motherless monkeys*)
5. Conditions and expectations are often placed on loving and being loved. <u>Is this OK?</u>
    a. Are there different kinds of love?
        (1. Brainstorm different kinds of love and write them down.
        (2. Attach names of people for whom you/your group feels these kinds of love.
    b. Make a list of people whom you used to love but stopped loving.
        (1. What happened to change your feelings?
        (2. What feelings do you have towards these people now?
        (3. How would you, or did you, take away love (or vice versa – did someone take love away from you)?
        (4. What would have to change in order for you to love them again?
        (5. What do your friends have to do in order for you to love them?
        (6. What do you think you have to do in order to be loved by: grandparents, aunts and uncles, parents, siblings, girlfriends, boyfriends, teachers, classmates?
6. Why do people marry? Why do people not marry? Do people have to marry when they fall in love? What happens to people who love each other?

7. Can people love people who are different than themselves?
    a. What makes people different from one another? What about the differences between boys and girls; parents and children; you now and you last year? How are you different from the person sitting next to you? Is it okay to be different?
    b. How are "different" people the same? Have you ever met someone you felt close to and also felt different from? When? What was it like for you?
8. What is your favorite song about love (or poem, or saying)? Share it.

At a workshop I was leading in Australia, an 18-year-old man with muscular dystrophy asked, "I haven't much time left and I want to make love. What do I have to do to get to that phase in a relationship?"

We used that opportunity to review the stages one goes through in getting to know someone in a relationship, progressing to sexual intimacy. As a group, we brainstormed the sequence of events, from sharing common interests, to sharing feelings, to expressing feelings of caring and affection, to kissing and petting, to going steady, and learning about birth control and sexual responsibility.

---

* "Rock-a-Bye-Baby," A Time-Life Documentary Film

SEX ROLES

The following are specific objectives for learning:
1. To become aware that everyone has both masculine and femanine characteristics and qualities in themselves.
2. To notice the difference beween masculine and feminine behaviors.
3. To understand that we are more than our roles in life.
4. To notice how different segments of society, different relationships, have/place different expectations of/on us.
5. To learn ways to express our intentions more clearly.

BEING MASCULINE, BEING FEMININE, BEING BOTH

How does each person express the feminine side and the masculine side of their character? To understand and accept the feminine parts of a woman or a man, it is important to understand those feminine parts in yourself. To understand the masculine side of a woman or a man, understand the masculine side or parts of yourself. If you allow yourself to understand and accept all of these parts, you will be that much closer to experiencing yourself as a "whole person".

Maturity level: age 13+

Activity: Role-playing masculine and feminine activities:
How would someone "feminine" do the following? How would someone "masculine" do the following? (These are play-acting activities for your class.)
1. Hammer a nail.
2. Arrange flowers.
3. Look in the mirror.
4. Tell a joke.
5. Throw a ball.
6. Drink.
7. Eat / use a napkin.
8. Cry.
9. Laugh.
10. Talk about their feelings.
11. Show affection.
12. Express being hurt physically, emotionally.
13. Walk.
14. Look at their fingernails.

Activity: Listing Expectations Associated With Sex Roles:
1. List experiences and feelings associated with the following:
    a. My mother always said, "Boys should…"
    b. Because I am a boy, I didn't have to…"
    c. My mother/father always said, "Boys shouldn't…"
    d. My father/mother always said, "Ladies don't…"
    e. My father/mother always said, "Ladies should…"
    f. Because I am a girl, I don't have to…
    g. Because I am a girl, I have to…

2. Write the male counterpart to these female words:
    a. Nymphomaniac (ex: "stud")
    b. Old maid
    c. Spinster
    d. Broad
    e. Chick
    f. Shrew, etc.

Do both counterparts have equal status? Which are more of a put down? Create some male words and find female counterparts. (Not so easy!)

Activity: Tell Me Who You Are?
   Maturity level: age 15+
(Developed by Dr. Stanley Krippner of Miamonedes Medical Center in Brooklyn, New York.)
1. Each person has nine small pieces of paper.
2. Answer the question: "Who am I?" in nine different ways on a separate piece of paper (age, sex, profession, self-image, role, etc.).
3. Complete all answers and arrange answers in sequence by order of importance to you, description number 9 being the least important.
4. Begin with description number 9.
    a. Leader addresses each person by saying: "Tell me who you are."
    b. Participant answers: "I am _____" (number 9).
    c. Leader responds: "Consider what life would be like for you if you were not _____" (number 9).
5. Leader moves to each participant and does number 9 again.
6. Proceed with number 8, then number 7, etc.
7. By the time you reach number 3 or number 2 you may start to notice the existence of something more to you than just these externals.
8. Experience that awareness.

THE MAN IN THE GLASS
Janet Zuckerman

When you get what you want in your struggle for yourself
    And the world makes you king for a day
Just go to a mirror and look at yourself
    And see what that person has to say.

For it isn't your mother or father or wife
    Whose judgment upon you must pass,
The person whose verdict counts most in your life
    Is the one staring back from the glass.

Now, some people can call you a straight shootin' chum
    And think you're a wonderful guy,

But the man in the glass says you're only a bum
    If you won't look him straight in the eye.

He's the one to please, never mind all the rest
For he's with you clear up to the end,
And you've passed your most dangerous and difficult test
If the man in the glass can at least be your friend.

You can fool the whole world down the pathway of years
And get lots of pats on the back as you pass,
But your final reward will be heartaches and tears
If you cheat the man in the glass.

Activity: "Wants Me To Be" Chart:
Maturity level: age 13+

The students concentrate on each square and decide (whatever first pops into mind) what they feel each person or institution wants them to be. Then state who you really are and whose life you are living. Do this in groups of two or three.

WANTS ME TO BE
(Adjectives, Activities, Vocations, etc.)

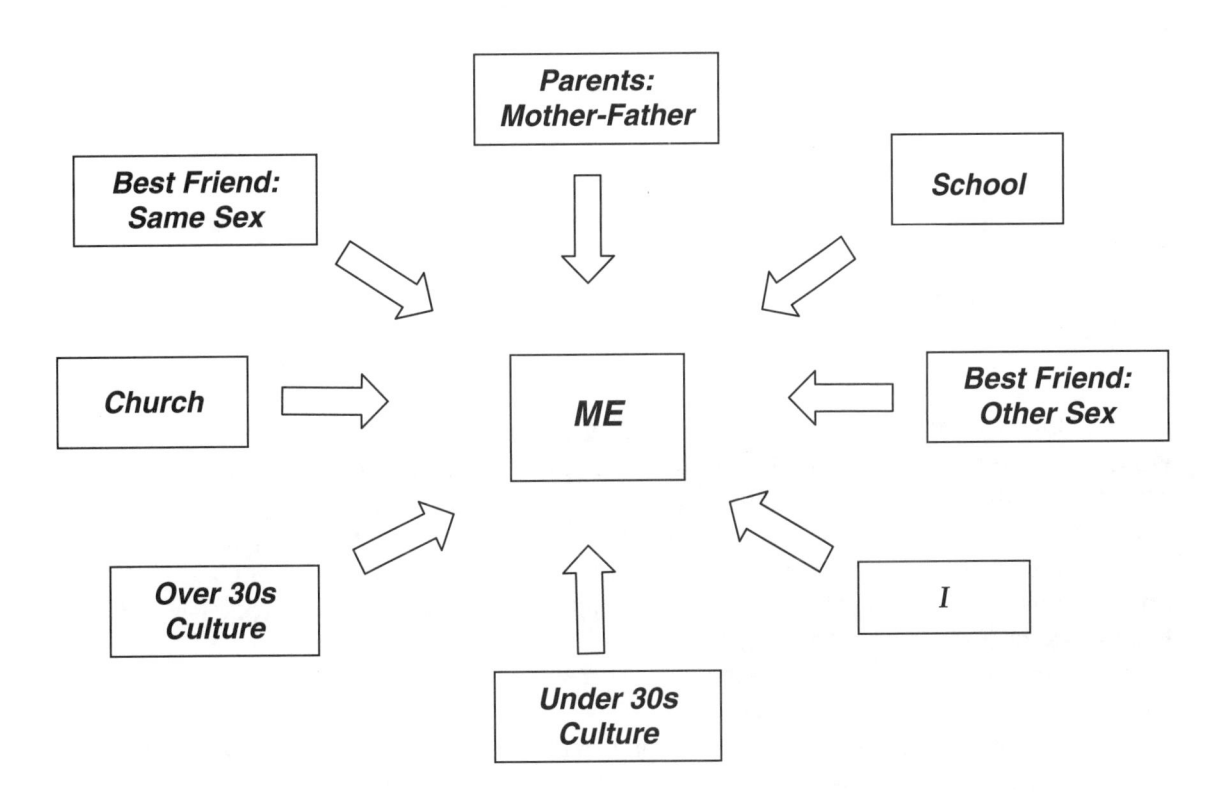

```
        Parents:
      Mother-Father
                          
Best Friend:                      School
Same Sex
        ↘        ↓        ↙
                                  Best Friend:
Church    ⇒     ME     ⇐          Other Sex
        ↗        ↑        ↖
Over 30s                           I
Culture
        Under 30s
        Culture
```

Activity: Collage

The advertising media reinforce traditional sex-role images. Class members collect advertisements appealing to sex-role images, male chauvinism, etc., and make a class collage.

SEMANTICS

Here is an exercise in word use that can quickly transform your perception of how you create your own moods, limitations, attitudes and beliefs. Bring these techniques to your group.

CAN'T

Eliminate the word *can't* from your vocabulary and substitute *won't*. For example, "I can't keep my promises," becomes "I won't keep my promises." "I can't stop drinking," becomes "I won't stop drinking." Both means of expressing the thought might be true. The use of *won't*, however, creates much more of a sense of personal power and clearly identifies who is the real source of decision making and who is responsible. *Can't* is, after all, a pretty weak excuse. *Won't* is much more assertive and is really much more honest. Even if you think that you really mean "can't," use "won't" for a while. Notice what it teaches you.

TRY

Substitute the word "do" for the word "try." Here's an experiment. Put a pencil on the table in front of you. Now, with all your might, *"try"* to move it. It doesn't move. Sometimes there is more resistance in "trying" than in actually doing the task. You are *trying* to move it of course, but you are not necessarily *moving* it. "Trying" to do something is semantically different than "doing" something. Now instead, just *move* it. It moves! It's much better to eliminate the word "try" when you are encouraging someone to perform a task. Say: "Move it," or "Do your best to do it." This way you are expressing your belief in that individual's ability to perform the task. You are expressing confidence in that person.

BUT

The word *but* is used in order to negate that which was said immediately beforehand. "I'd love to go out with you tomorrow but I'm too tired," means, "I don't want to go out with you tomorrow and I'm giving you an excuse." Instead of *but*, use the word *and*. This little word switch will help to keep you honest with yourself. When your group uses this technique, the communication becomes a lot simpler, less ambiguous and more honest.

SHOULD

Notice when and how you use the word *should*. Stop using it and find a better word. Ask yourself, "Who runs the *should* machine?" That is, who is the authority who created the *should?* Either use the name of that authority in your conversation or else acknowledge that you yourself actually are that authority. It may be that you are using *should* as a method of coercion on yourself or on another, to not do something that may be attractive or to do something that is unattractive. Be aware of that. Prof. Sylvia Hacker says, "Don't *should* on yourself."

WHY

Ask "why?" less often. Use some other substitute such as "how?" *Why* is a valid tool for scientific investigation. When it comes to human communication, especially the communication of feelings; reasons, excuses, explanations and justifications are usually of little value in enhancing closeness, intimacy and love. *Why* invites a volume of intellectualization when there is simply a feeling that needs to be shared. When a happy bride exclaims, "I'm so happy!" imagine someone asking her, "Why?" And imagine what she'd look like if she actually tried to answer with scientific accuracy. She would sit down, become serious, maybe take out a pencil and jot down notes. Meanwhile, the happiness has gone away. Romeo asked, "*How* do I love thee, let me count the ways." He didn't ask, "*Why* do I love you? Maybe I don't."

FEELING, RECOGNIZING AND DEALING WITH EMOTIONS

EMBRACING YOUR FAMILY OF FEELINGS

Experiencing emotions is an important part of feeling alive. Your feelings are a needed source of inner guidance. Discouraging yourself or others from honoring feelings will often result in regrets. Even when feelings are unpleasant it is usually better to face them and feel something rather than block them and feel nothing or feel numb or dead.

Each feeling competes for your attention like siblings do in a family. Get to know each of your feelings; become friends with them.

The suggestions and ideas described in this guide are for a process that is as much your own as teacher or group leader as it is for your students or clients. This is a process of watching, becoming aware of, and taking responsibility (*response ability*) for feelings, starting with your *own* feelings. You are the model. The chances are that the clearer and more honest you are with your own experiences, the more you will be imitated; thus, the more response-able (able to respond) your students will become. As a model you are not looking to make the class or group to become you. Only you can be you. Rather, you are the model for a process of self-disclosure, self-respect, awareness, sharing, trust and responsibility. This attitude is communicated to your students by your natural behavior and learned naturally by your students without their thinking about it.

The following are specific objectives for learning:
1. To become aware of our feelings.
2. To learn to identify the emotions we are feeling.
3. To develop verbal skills in expressing our feelings appropriately.
4. To interpret facial expressions showing emotions.
5. To become aware of situations which cause specific or general emotional reactions.
6. To interpret different body language expressing emotions of happiness, unhappiness anger and fear.
7. Interpreting another's emotions as that other person's own feelings without taking it personally.
8. To become aware of emotions changing as situations change.
9. To become aware of emotions expressed with different tones of voice.
10. To recognize and express different ways people respond to emotions and situations.
11. To recognize and express the consequences of different emotional reactions.
12. To become aware of music creating moods for emotion.

Having a feeling never needs to be defended. Feelings are each individual's indicator of what is going on inside. "You shouldn't feel that way," is never a legitimate statement. The fact that you do feel something is reason enough to honor those emotions. That doesn't mean that you need to hold on to that feeling. Remember to allow yourself to move on to better feelings. Myron Glatt reminds us of this by asking, "Would you rather be right or happy?" (See page 72 on Letting Go of Emotions)

Sometimes people really don't know how they feel until they actually hear themselves (or another person) describe what is going on inside. Sometimes different feelings overlap. For example, feeling disappointed or abandoned could also be described as feeling fearful, unhappy or even angry.

The following activities are designed to develop verbal skills for the process of feeling, recognizing and dealing with emotions. Adapt the exercises to meet the specific needs, interests, intellectual level, maturity and general readiness level of your individual students/clients and yourself.

WORDS THAT HELP US DESCRIBE AND RECOGNIZE HOW WE FEEL

Maturity level: age 10+

If you or your students/clients need help finding the word or words that best describe how they feel, the following lists will be helpful. Often, when we can define how we feel, we gain control of our feelings and then feel more empowered. To define is to limit. Thus, the process of defining feelings is an effective way to overcome or move beyond negative or unpleasant feelings.

LEARN WORDS TO EXPRESS HAPPINESS

Hand out a list of "Words of Happiness" to each student. Students check the words with which they are familiar either through experience or general use. If students cannot read, ask class to raise their hands if the word read aloud by the teacher or assistant is familiar. Talk about the words in the list applying them to experiences in school, work or personal life. Brainstorm more "Words of Happiness" with the class' participation.

Words of HAPPINESS: I am feeling...

touched	satisfied	optimistic/hopeful
pleased	relieved	bliss
comfortable	restored	loved/loving
content	cheerful	forgiving/forgiven
blessed	delighted	helpful
merry	joyful	whole/complete
good	pleasure	enchanted

Activity: Explore emotional situations involving happiness.

1. Have the students close their eyes and think back, as far back as they need, "back when you last felt happy, really happy. There you were. Picture yourself there." Students answer each question either with a partner or in a small group.
    a. What did your eyes look like? Your eyebrows? Your mouth? Your cheeks? Your shoulders?
    b. What sounds were you making to express how you felt?
    c. Where were you?
    d. Who was there?
    e. What were you doing?
    f. What was going on around you?
    g. How do you know you were happy?
2. Another happiness set of questions: "Think back to your first favorite teacher or friend. How did you feel about her (him)? What did your teacher or friend do that made you feel special? What was it that you did that made you feel special?"
3. Describe a situation that has or would make you feel happy. Perhaps someone expressed something special to you either verbally or nonverbally.
    a. How did or would they express the message to you?
    b. Find a word in the list to say exactly how you felt.
    c. How have or would you express to another person a happy feeling in a specific situation, verbally and nonverbally?
    d. Explore different tones of voice in expressing emotions in the list.
    e. Explore different facial expressions people use to express happiness words nonverbally.

f. Explore different gestures people can use to express feelings listed. (You may enjoy using a game-like structure similar to charades. One person, or several at a time with a partner, may choose one out of five of the list to communicate with facial expressions or body gestures while the class tries to guess which feeling word is being communicated.)
4. List four headings on the board similar or equivalent to: "Ecstatically happy!!!" "Delighted!!" "Pleased!" and "Content." Students share experiences or situations that bring on each feeling and how that feeling was expressed and received and experienced as a bodily feeling. For example: "I told my parents how I really felt about their decision that I couldn't go out with my friends. Then they changed their minds and said I could go! I was so ecstatically happy that I hugged them both and they kissed me back."

LEARN WORDS TO EXPRESS UNHAPPINESS
Hand out a list of "Words of Unhappiness" to each student. Students check the words with which they are familiar. Let the students discuss the words on the list and add others.

Words of UNHAPPINESS: I am feeling...

uneasy	tearful	guilty
bored	grief	sorry
tired	lost	miserable
worn out	abandoned	regretful
sad	gloomy	crushed
drained	excluded	rejected
heavy inside	helpless	hurt
depressed	hopeless	numb
disappointed	pessimistic	bitter
lonely	burdened	obsessed
left out	bad	doubtful

Activity: Explore emotional situations involving unhappiness.
Refer to page 67 (feelings of happiness) and apply the emotional situations to feelings of unhappiness.

LEARN WORDS TO EXPRESS FEAR
Hand out a list of "Words of Fear" to each student. Let the students discuss the words on the list and add others.

Words of FEAR: I am feeling...

fearful	cautious	afraid
blamed	out of control	repelled
caught	pushed/hurried	distrustful
embarrassed	vulnerable	hesitant
no self-confidence	threatened	misunderstood
shy	anxious	suspicious
nervous	judged	helpless
rejected	worried	nervous
jumpy	panicky	freaked out

Sometimes anger and fear are interchangeable feelings. Sharing fearful concerns or situations may bring up problems that involve sexual exploitation. Reassure your student or client that you're glad that they brought the situation to your attention and that you will discuss it with them in private, later.

Activity: Explore emotional situations involving fear using drawing, pantomime and discussion.
1. Think about a time that you felt frightened. (Where was it? When? Who was with you? What happened?)
    a. Using a single extra-large sheet of paper, have the group draw a picture about this experience (Do this all together to avoid artistic comparisons.) Colors as well as shapes can express feelings.
    b. Do a pantomime or let one part of your body (hand, eyes, foot, etc.) show fear. This can be done individually or as a group.
    c. Add sound (not necessarily words) to the pantomime or movement.
    d. Point out that fear is often unnecessary. Fear stands for **False Evidence Appearing Real**. Fear is often the result of misinterpreting a situation, feeling anxious before we have the facts, having catastrophic expectations; for instance, fearing that someone will stop loving you if you express yourself honestly.
    e. To whom can you go when you're feeling fearful or freaked out?
    f. Dr. Fritz Perls, the father of Gestalt Therapy, stated that "anxiety is the distance between now and then."

LEARN WORDS TO EXPRESS ANGER
Hand out a list of "Words of Anger" to each student. Let the students discuss the words on the list and add others. Dr. Fritz Perls says: "Depression is often anger turned inward." When his patients felt depressed he would ask them, "With whom are you angry?" or "What is making you feel angry?"

Words of ANGER: I am feeling...

angry	hurt	depressed
disappointed	controlled	rejected
annoyed	unsafe/insecure	impatient
disturbed	provoked	frustrated
tied up inside	pushed	rushed
ignored	confined	guilty
abandoned	"I must protect myself"	manipulated/used
mislead	betrayed	jealous/excluded
rage	vindictive/ "I'll show you"	abused
hostile	upset	furious

Activity: Explore emotional situations involving anger.
Suggested questions for discussion sessions:
1. Close your eyes and remember back to a time when you felt really angry.
    a. When was it? Where were you?
    b. Who was with you?
    c. What happened?
    d. How did you feel?
    e. How do you feel about it now?
    f. What would you do differently?
2. Read or tell or show a picture about an emotional situation (either made-up or experienced by yourself or the students, from a newspaper, a magazine or a book). Each student decides on the most specific feeling words to describe how the person experiencing the situation may have felt. (This process is called empathy)

3. Brainstorm with the group situations that get them angry. This works best if all ideas are accepted with unconditional appreciation and then written on the board or onto large pieces of paper for everyone to see. After listing all the ideas, brainstorm different ways to respond to or handle those situations. Write down and discuss the consequences of each solution offered. Be creative!

   For example:
   Someone is staring at you on the bus.
   Solution:
   Say with a smile: "Gee you stare good!" (and wink).
   Consequence:
   You complimented them and broke the ice and perhaps made them laugh and feel good.
   They stopped staring at you.
   You might become friends.

4. You or a student reads or makes up a short statement loaded with emotional content directed toward the students. For example: "You can't do anything right!" Each student identifies how he or she felt upon hearing this and how the person who said it may have felt. When someone is angry, they may have the right to be angry but that doesn't give them the right to be cruel.

5. Discuss friends having different opinions and having arguments. Point out that just because two people argue, it doesn't mean they don't like or love each other. And just because they don't argue doesn't automatically mean that they do like or love each other.

6. Pantomime: How am I feeling? In response to the following suggested situations (use situations that have come up for your group in the past) the group guesses the feeling acted out.

7. Hold discussion sessions to consider the following: "How do you think you would feel and what would you do or say? What would your face, your shoulders, your hands, your body, express when:
   a. someone criticizes how you look?"
   b. someone cuts in front of you in line?"
   c. someone of the same (or opposite) sex accidentally walks into the bathroom while you are sitting on the toilet?"
   d. someone bumps into you accidentally?"
   e. your friend accuses you, 'Why did you say bad things about me?'"
   f. your friends won't let you join them?"

Anger Can Be Your Strength and Ally

There was a time in my life when I felt a lot of anger and it kept popping up when least expected. I believed that anger was bad so I pushed it away, avoided it, denied it or buried it. Anything to get rid of it.

One day I was at a gathering and was having a conversation with a young man. As I spoke I noticed that his eyes seemed to be studying my face. "Your face keeps moving with anger," he said.

I didn't know whether to feel angry or defensive or to flee. "What do you mean?" I asked.

He repeated, "Your face keeps moving with anger."

I felt like stamping my foot and saying, "I'm not angry!" Instead I had the good sense to say, "Thank you for sharing that information with me."

Later as I drove home I kept hearing his words and thinking about his message. It rang deep inside with truth and I didn't know what to do about it. I followed my instincts and parked the car. I closed my eyes and invited my anger to speak to me. My anger came forth in my mind like a wild and powerful lion roaring at me. "You embrace love, joy, happiness, sorrow and even fear, but me you push away repeatedly. That's why I have to keep your face moving. And that's why I act out and show up at all the wrong times and places. It's because you push me away and never listen and acknowledge my presence. I've always been there for you whenever you needed me. I've always given you strength, but are you there for me? No! Me, you push away, bury and deny."

I felt myself soften to this plea of my new friend and ally. I extended my arms to my imaginary roaring lion and spoke tearfully and sincerely. "You're right! You have always been there when I needed you. You have always given me strength. I promise I will never push you away. I promise I will treasure you my friend, my anger, and I will be here for you as you have been here for me." I then witnessed my roaring lion contently transform into a purring kitten in my mind's embrace.

What I learned is to accept my family of feelings inside me. I learned that they can work together to serve me and others. When I combine my love with my anger I have the strength of courage.

LETTING GO OF EMOTIONS

If you are feeling "stuck" in an emotion, what are some ways to change it?
   Maturity level: 12+
Here are some suggestions. Some of these activities require a relatively sophisticated group. Use your judgement.
1. Identify how you feel (state it or show it nonverbally).
2. Take responsibility for your own feelings. Take responsibility for changing how you feel. Don't get stuck blaming others. For example, say: "I am feeling ____," rather than: "You make me feel _____."
3. Put yourself in the other person's shoes (place). Imagine how they might be feeling in their situation.
4. Then express how you feel directly to the person it concerns (verbally) or in writing (a letter) or indirectly to a mutual friend or to a pillow or a punching bag (see "Yes-No Process"). Have a good cry or laugh.
5. Write this statement clearly on a piece of paper and sign it:

> *I have just created a thought or feeling myself. Its effects will wear off. I don't have to believe everything I think. The thought isn't me.*
> *I am _____ (signature)*

6. Allow yourself to let go of the feeling. Imagine yourself holding on to a feeling as you clutch a towel as tightly as you can. Then let go of the feeling as you let go of the towel.
7. **Learning to forgive others and yourself is essential for mental health.** You may be justified in feeling angry. "Forgiveness does not mean 'What you did is OK to me.' It simply means 'I am no longer willing to carry around pain in response to your actions.' When we hold unforgiveness in our hearts we only punish ourselves... You don't need to forgive the action, just the person, so that you can be at peace..."* and

---

* from "Healing With the Angels Oracle Cards," by Doreen Virtue, Ph.D.

move on to feeling good about yourself. Some people refuse to forgive others in the misguided attempt to hold on to control over those persons. They believe that if they forgive someone, that someone will be "off the hook." *Forgiveness is for giving to yourself!*

8. Forgive and Release Visualization:**
    a. Close your eyes, take a few deep breaths.
    b. Imagine the person you wish to forgive and the feelings you wish to release.
    c. Imagine yourself saying to this person: "I return to you that which is yours." Then say to yourself: "I return to myself that which is mine."
    d. Imagine cutting the cords that connect you with them as you say: "I release you and forgive you with love, I release myself and forgive myself with love."
    e. Repeat this visualization several times until you feel released and free of the hold they (the feeling or the person) had on you.

9. Six questions to transform disappointment into a positive lesson:
    a. What did I expect?
    b. What actually happened?
    c. What is there to accept that may be difficult to accept?
    d. What is the lesson to be learned?
    e. What have I learned that I can teach others?
    f. What would I do differently next time?

10. Coping: Dr. Stella Resnick says, "Often when we decide to **"cope"** with an emotionally draining (and perhaps physically draining) situation we are choosing to live with the unlivable or the unbearable because we are avoiding making a decision to change. We take tranquilizers or other medication to **cope** when what we really need is to change our situation, change our circumstances, as soon as possible."

11. Change your situation.

12. Experience music as creating and changing moods.
    a. Each student brings in music that creates different moods (happy, sad, scary, angry).
    b. Play the music and each student will compare with others the mood or emotion they experience.

13. Dance and shake off the feelings. Let any part of your body that can dance (eyebrows, eyes, head, tongue, shoulders, arms, one finger, big toe, any part) move to music. Liberate yourself!

14. Read this poem of appreciation:

A POEM
(Author anonymous)

I am here for you always,
I am beyond attachment,
I am beyond sadness,
I am beyond fear,
I exist in and as radiant love.

Come to me in your sadness
And I will hold you in the arms of your mother.

** from "Healing With Love," by Leonard Laskow, M.D.

Come to me in your fear
And I will care for you, guide you and protect you.
Come to me when your lover leaves you
And I will be your lover.
Come to me when you are torn by guilt
And I shall lift the veil of falsehood and make you whole.
Come to me when you fear you have failed
And I will show you the true magnificence of your success.

I am your golden guide,
The shining priestess of your temple,
The living light of your soul.
I am surrounded by the holiest beings in the universe.
They are your helpers.

You alone can meet me here.
It is through you that others know me,
Hear my wisdom,
Feel my infinite love,
Be comforted and healed.

Your work is to free yourself so that I may embody your life.
I give you all that I am.

All of my mystical power awaits your command.
All of my love longs to flow through your heart.
All of my knowledge I bequeath to you.
Speak it! Now!
I am with you always.
Bring me forth
Oh, my Self.

EXPERIENCING ONESELF THROUGH THE SENSES

Helen Keller said, *"In order to attain his highest education the child must be persistently encouraged to extract joy and constructive interest from sight, hearing, touch, smell and taste... If a mother puts as much gentle art into this delicate fostering of all his physical powers as she does into the task of preserving his health... not only will he reach a well-ordered stewardship of his senses, he will also have the best chance of spiritual maturity... Every person, every group thus excellently equipped for living, is the greatest possible contribution to humanity."*

The following are specific objectives for learning:
1. To experience an awareness of how we and others respond to various fragrances, odors, smells.
2. To explore and experience sensory clues in identifying objects.
3. To explore and experience different sensations of touch on one's body.

4. To encourage body exploration to discover how and where stimulation is experienced.
5. To experience different ways in which one touches a friend.
6. To express how one feels when one is being touched or touching another person.
7. To experience nonverbal communication through touching.
8. To experience one's own sensuality through touching and being touched.
9. To experience, mindfully, tasting different textures, flavors, spices.
10. To experience what smell and taste have in common.
11. To become aware of how to respond to visual input.
12. To become aware of how to control one's visual image.
13. To express feelings about body image.
14. To become aware of how to project body image to others.
15. To experience classmates as sensual human beings.
16. To share experiences verbally and nonverbally.
17. To experience one's body in new ways.
18. To gain self-awareness and responsibility for one's appearance.

From the moment you were born you were a sensual human being. You sensed the temperature of the outside world, you sensed the bright lights in the room, you sensed the warmth of your mother's arms, the smoothness and softness of her breast next to your cheek. You tasted and sucked anything you could bring to your mouth. You sensed the sound of your mother's voice soothing you. You sensed the warmth, smell and texture of your feces in your diaper. You spent hours exploring: touching, smelling, tasting, watching, listening to your own body and the body of the person holding you. Each of us has had this natural gift from the very beginning of our life... and still do!

EXPERIENCING OURSELVES THROUGH THE SENSE OF SMELL

Maturity level: age 7+
1. Each student brings samples of things found outside, produced by nature, to share with the class.
    a. Bring things that smell pleasant.
    b. Bring things that smell unpleasant.
2. Each student brings to class perfumes, essences, soaps, deodorants, shampoo, hair sprays, hair tonic, etc.
    a. Which fragrance would you enjoy smelling on a male? Female? Why?
    b. What kinds of smells make you want to get close to a person? Can you tell if someone washes regularly?
    c. What kinds of smells do you move away from?
        (1. Breath? (What odors are appealing, or unappealing, e.g., cigarette smoke, brushed teeth, candy, alcohol?)
        (2. Sweat? (This is not necessarily unpleasant, although it may be so if it is stale. For instance, fresh perspiration from physical activity need not be attractive or unattractive. It is just there. Perspiration from fear may smell bad. Sweaty clothing worn the next day may smell unpleasant.)
        (3. Urine? (Persons with catheters or Foley bags may appreciate learning how they are being perceived olfactorily. Maybe there is a leak that can be corrected.)
        (4. Menstrual fluid? (Is there an odor during the period? Is it just inadequate attention to changing napkins or underwear? Maybe there is no odor; that's reassuring to know, too.)

3. Each member of the group brings his or her favorite smell to share (in jars).
4. Categorize or match jars according to the odor of their contents.

EXPERIENCING OURSELVES THROUGH THE SENSE OF TOUCH

Close your eyes and feel the air against your skin. Feel the clothing against your skin.

Activity: Touch-discrimination exercise:
   Maturity level: 5+
1. Blindfold everyone participating.
2. Objects of varying sizes, shapes and textures are handed out (or drawn from a sack individually), one to each person.
3. Record who has which object for reference.
4. Each person is asked to explore the object in as many ways possible while blindfolded.
    a. Explore and describe its shape, weight, texture, taste, smell, temperature.
    b. From what material is it made?
5. Objects are randomly placed on a table and each person then feels for his or her own object and takes it back.
6. Describe how each one figured out which was one's own. (Participants are still blindfolded.)
7. Put objects back on table randomly.
8. Remove blindfolds. Each person finds his or her own object using only eyesight for identification.
9. Discussion of experience:
    a. Which way of finding your object was best for you? Was it feeling or seeing? Why?
    b. Which was easier, more difficult?
    c. What do you think would have happened if you saw your object first?
    d. You may do exercise again in reverse order. (This also can be done by differentiating different spice odors or tastes).
10. Feel and discuss different textures on your fingers, face, feet, etc. Examples: a flower, velvet, sandpaper, a baby, an orange, a bird, a dog, paper, oils, washing your hands with soap, petroleum jelly, etc.
    a. How does each feel to you?
    b. How do you touch a flower? A baby? A pillow?
11. How do you touch a friend? An enemy? A stranger?
    a. To get their attention?
    b. To free yourself from each?
    c. To convey different messages?
12. Touch your own body in different ways:
    a. Tap with finger tips on head and face.
    b. Slap (with palms and fingers held flat):
        (1. Head, face, down entire body.
        (2. Chest while vocalizing "ahhh" getting louder and then softer, inhaling and exhaling deeply.
    c. Place hands apart on belly (close eyes for three minutes and follow your breath - the moving air, as it passes your nose, throat, lungs, diaphragm, belly).
    d. Experience squeezing your body with your hands.
    e. Experience a light touch, so light that you get goosebumps (face, neck, shoulder, arm-pit, chest, down to bottoms of feet).

13. Strong expressions of affection are more socially appropriate when expressed in private. Kissing (other than light kisses of greeting between good friends), fondling one another, necking, full body hugging and other affectionate touching that may be sexually oriented is not appropriate in public settings.
14. Discussion questions about affection:
    a. How did your family communicate "I love you," or "I like you," to you, to friends, to relatives?
    b. Who was the first peer for whom you remember feeling great affection? How was this expressed?
    c. Act out ways to touch affectionately (socially appropriately).

EXPERIENCING OURSELVES THROUGH THE SENSE OF TASTE

Maturity level: 7+

1. Blindfolded, identify different substances and textures of food by tasting. Discuss how one can tell a nonfood from a food.
2. Help each person understand that smell influences taste. Smell and taste different spices. Hold your nose tasting. Inhale through your nose, tasting. Exhale through your nose, tasting.
3. Explore the tastes of your own body. (How would you describe them?)
4. Everyone, mindfully, slowly and completely, chew a piece of bread (homemade, preferably; perhaps one of the students could prepare this treat) with their eyes closed, together.

EXPERIENCING OURSELVES THROUGH THE SENSE OF HEARING

Maturity level: 6+

1. Close your eyes. Relax. Listen to your own breathing.
2. Close your eyes, relax and listen to one sound in the room. Simply focus your hearing on that one sound. Listen to another sound. Listen to all the sounds. Listen to the first sound again.
3. Listen to your heartbeat. Listen to your classmates' heartbeats. (You may use a stethoscope or a mailing tube, or students may put their ear to other students' backs, or to the chest of male students.)
4. Identify pleasant and unpleasant sounds.
5. Identify pleasant and unpleasant voice qualities and volumes.
6. Take turns humming and guessing songs.
7. How can we tell if someone is listening - not listening?
8. Experiment with speaking or singing with different voice qualities, pitch, pace and volume. (Try variations on a short story or joke.)
9. Someone hides a loudly clicking clock or timer. Others try to find it.

EXPERIENCING OURSELVES THROUGH THE SENSE OF VISION

Maturity level: 12+

1. Become a camera. Close your eyes. Then open them for a moment and close them again. You just took a snapshot of whatever you saw. Describe what you saw with your eyes still shut. Then open them.
2. Explore different interpretations of a picture of action (perhaps a pantomime of visual communication).
3. Consider how we present our own visual image with group feed-back. What is our body communicating?

a. Explore different facial expressions.
   b. Explore different postures and positioning.
   c. Experiment with different gestures.
   d. Experiment with different movements and mannerisms. (What looks good? What looks and sounds weird? How can we improve?)
   e. What are we saying with our body language?
   f. Notice where you locate your body in relation to others (close, distant).
   g. Use eye contact.
   h. Observe dress, style, fit, colors and general grooming and neatness.
      (1. What hair and clothing styles and colors look good on you?
      (2. Bring in a full-length mirror and invite a style and color specialist from your local beauty school to do make-over consultations with the group.

   In our workshop there was a 26-year-old client. Whenever he was happy or excited he would clap his hands and rock back-and-forth while standing in a posture of someone repeatedly bowing. He had the chance to see his own behavior on the video monitor. We pointed this out to him asking him how he could look better. He made suggestions for his own alternative behavior. Several months later he went out on his first date and he came up to us afterwards, very pleased with himself. He told us about the date and how he didn't "act weird" and stood straight and tall and what a good time he had.

   Children and teenagers (and even adults), whether disabled or not, are very aware of behavior and whether or not it is "weird" or "funny" or just not appropriate for their peer group. What people who are slow learners or who have other cognitive disabilities often lack is the ability or opportunity to observe themselves for the same "weirdness." It's like the commercial advertisement for mouthwash that tells you that even your best friend won't tell you. If your best friend won't tell you, how can you ever learn? If the best friend is a trusted teacher or peer in a safe environment, using video feedback, the student usually responds appreciatively to the information. You can empower your student or client even more by encouraging him/her to be the first to come up with solutions, ideas or suggestions for behavioral changes.

4. One's signature is another visual representation in the world. Give each person (including yourself) a piece of plain crisp, clean stationary, a sharpened pencil and a comfortable place to write. Each person spends time enjoying the pleasure of writing his or her name. Write it several times in different ways with different strokes. Enjoy writing your own name. Enjoy the way you represent yourself to the world. Enjoy being you. Each person holds up their best signature and says, "My name is _____, and this is my signature." The group gives applause of appreciation.
5. Each person stands in front of a mirror and describes the person they see from the outside and inside. If anyone has difficulty describing himself, that person may invite two or three friends in the group to do the description (outside = physical appearance; inside = the feeling self).
6. Discussion session: What we like about each other's visual image and how we could improve ourselves (allow extra time for this subject).

(Note: The teacher or group leader encourages everyone to concentrate on positive personal attitudes and encourages the attitude that each person can enhance their own self-concept.)

Activity: Improving the image our body offers to the world.
Maturity level: age 13+

Explain: Your body represents you in society. You are all more than a body. We all know that! Each of you is a beautiful, sensitive, aware spirit housed in a body. Your body is your temple where you live. You are free to treat your body with respect and love, or not.

1. What are ways in which you show love and respect to your body?
2. What are the ways in which you don't? You have choices of how you want to present your physical image to the world in which you live. These choices will determine how well you fit into society, the mainstream of life.
3. What are some of the choices you have considered and acted on?
4. Which are the choices you considered and didn't act on? (Video recording is an excellent medium for feedback on body image.)

TRAINING STAFF AND PARENTS AS SEX EDUCATORS

The following are specific objectives for learning:
1. Methods to introduce to parents the importance of sex education for their disabled daughters or sons.
2. To learn what parents' concerns and needs are regarding sex education.
3. To learn what parents' fears are regarding sex edcuation
4. To demythologize beliefs regarding physically challenged people and their sexuality.
5. To learn how to train parents to become effective sex educators.
6. How to grain support from parents for your own sex education program.

Sex has been a subject of interest and fascination ever since woman and man began. Although sex may be a "natural" function, open discussion of sexual matters is often difficult and threatening or taboo. Comparison, titillation, embarrassment, shame and misunderstanding all too often replace productive and informative communication (whether with sex partners, friends, counselors, teachers, physicians, clergy, parents or children).

When one's car is not running properly or one's arm is aching, it is a simple matter to ask a friend or professional for advice. But when one has a question about one's own sexuality, even if he or she can ask somebody, there may not be someone around willing to answer. Are *you* someone comfortable and willing to listen and answer sexual questions? How are you feeling right now, imagining yourself in this situation?

The time to talk to your son or daughter about sex is best started informally when they are young.

When I was ten years old, the older girls on the block wouldn't let me hang out with them when they giggled about sex. It irked me to be pushed away so I persisted until they relented and said, "OK. You can hear us talk about sex but only if you can find out how babies are made."

I ran to my mother and she nervously explained that the stork brought the baby to the parents.

I ran back, told the girls and they laughed at me. I angrily ran back to my mother accusing her of lying to me. She sighed and said as she gestured with her beautiful hands, "God plants a seed and from the seed a baby grows."

I ran back to the older girls and again they laughed at me. I ran back to my mother and I was livid! I felt like the laughing stock of my neighborhood! I demanded that she tell me the truth. She said, "I can't. Go ask your Auntie Millie."

I ran upstairs to ask my mother's sister, telling her all the lies I had been told and Auntie Millie told me about a man putting his penis in a woman's "duckie" (that's what my family called the vagina) and I turned green and felt like vomiting. I couldn't look at my Auntie Millie I was so disgusted by the concept (and obviously too young).

I ran throughout the neighborhood to track down the older girls and found them at the Homewood Theatre watching a movie. They didn't want to be distracted from watching the movie but they saw I had to tell them my disturbing finding. From the row behind I whispered into the ear of the oldest girl what Auntie Millie told me. Not taking her eyes off the movie screen, chomping on her popcorn and waving me away at the same time, she said, "You finally got it right, that's how it's done."

I got it right but I felt sick and disappointed and lost all desire to hang out with the older girls again. I had wanted to be part of their laughter and excitement but I wasn't ready for what it was all about. So I forgot about it until I was older and ready to talk about it with girls my own age.

When I was a young adult and I came home from a date, my mother usually waited up for me. She looked forward to hearing about my date. I knew that what she wanted to hear was how I went about refusing my date's sexual advances. She would repeat how she handled my Dad when he tried and because of that he married my mother instead of the other girls who were "easy." She would always remind me: "Why buy the cow if you can get the milk free?" I learned that I would lose my mother's trust if I shared my sexual experiences with her. I knew her limits.

This insight was brought back years later when we were conducting a workshop in Australia. The young adult clients and their parents sat in a circle as each client was asked who they would talk to about their sex lives. Not one client reported that they would go to their parent(s).

After the clients left the circle a number of the parents reported their disappointment that their son/daughter did not say they would come to them to talk about sex. Upon further discussion I asked each parent, "Did/do you talk about your sex life with your mother or father?" Every parent emphatically said "no, never!" When I asked "Why not?" they said "It doesn't feel right or comfortable to do so."

What we all realized is that their son or daughter's preference to not speak to them about their sex lives was actually normal and probably quite mature and appropriate. We sensed that if someone did share their intimate sexual experiences with their parents, it might be a sign that their son or daughter was not consenting to or ready for sex. It might indicate that they were being sexually exploited and asking them for help. If that were the case we reviewed how important it was never to blame them and reassure them that it wasn't their fault, that they are glad they shared what happened, reassuring them that they would protect them from further exploitation.

STAFF'S AND PARENTS' EXPECTATIONS OF TRAINING
This activity encourages the staff and/or the parents who wish to become sex educators to express what they hope to gain from the training and is an opportunity for the trainer to clarify what will be taking place.

Activity: Discussion
1. At the first meeting ask: "What do you want this training to include?"
    a. Write all the responses on large pieces of paper for later reference and review.

      b. You will find that some participants have only very general or vague questions in mind at this time, like "How do I teach sex education to my class?"
      c. Others may be less general, like "How do I teach my daughter with mental retardation about menstruation and feminine hygiene?"
      d. Still others may have very specific questions like "I have two young adults in my facility who want to have sex with each other but they are both severely physically disabled. What can or should I do to help them?"
2. Then ask: "What risks are you concerned about?"
3. "What do you fear could happen regarding the establishment of a sex education program?"
4. "What are potential risks of being part of this training group?"
5. Write down their responses too.

You will refer to these expectations, questions and concerns throughout the training. If some specific issues are not addressed, be sure to refer those persons to resources where they will find answers.

SELF-EXPECTATIONS AND CONCERNS OF A "SEX EDUCATOR"
Activity: Questionnaire
Participants may have concerns, doubts and anxiety about their ability to become competent sex educators. Use this activity to identify and define those concerns.

Invite participants to answer these questions (writing the answers in private):
1. List some of your strengths that will be helpful in your role as a sex educator.
2. List some of your weaknesses that could be a hindrance or a challenge to you in your role as a sex educator.
3. List two major students' needs in regards to self-esteem, social skills or sex information.
4. List five of your goals as a sex educator.
5. What is your biggest fear as a sex educator?

Break into small groups and discuss questions and answers. Each group has a scribe that summarizes the group discussion. Trainer brings groups together and processes information noting the groups' similarities and differences. Scribes from each group report their conclusions. Trainer addresses conclusions and decides what to focus on for the future. Use this Feeling Good About Yourself Guide and find the appropriate chapters for those issues.

Activity: Questions for a panel discussion:

Participants write out their own questions prior to panel discussion. Questions are handed to panel to review and panel decides who on the panel will answer them. Include these questions as well:

1. Why is it necessary to have a sex education program; from the perspective of the parent, the sex educator, the social worker, the facility, the church, the school, any other?
2. What are your concerns regarding sex education in a school setting and how it's taught in a school setting?
3. What topics would be important to cover in a sex education curriculum?
4. In what areas of a sex education program would you want input?

Note: always allow participants to give verbal feedback on the day's training.

RELATING TO PARENTS OF YOUNG ADULTS WITH DISABILITIES

A successful socialization and human sexuality program for children and young adults with special needs requires the consent and support of parents. This may offer you some challenging problems since these parents are often people who may see themselves as having gotten into trouble through their sexuality, the product of that activity being an abnormal child who may appear to be to them a reflection of *their* sexuality *together*. How do you reach stigmatized parents?

As coordinator of this program, you will be following the energy and interest of the parents at a comfortable pace. There are some programs, videos and guest speakers available through various agencies which will stimulate more discussion and openness. The *Feeling Good Playful Question Card Game* may provide a gentle and nonthreatening introduction to this issue (see Resources).

Familiarize parents with the Yes-No Process. They can be part of the team as they reinforce the program and support their son or daughter at home.

It's a good idea to collect individual objectives of what each person wants from being a part of a parents' self-esteem and sex education discussion group. Write their objectives on butcher paper and discuss them. Refer to these objectives throughout the program. If you help to establish an attitude of trust, parents are able to put aside their judgments about themselves and sexuality and merely watch themselves react to the various subjects. This way they get acquainted with their own attitudes, resistances, barriers and fears.

If this is a genuinely agreed-upon goal of each member in the parent group, you will have come a long way in changing the old attitudes that are directly affecting your students' and parents' lives. At this point you may consider forming an ongoing parent support group to provide an opportunity for parents to share common experiences and concerns. In this way they will be able to support each other as they unload themselves of guilt, resentment, fears and secrets with which they have burdened themselves for years. Remember, the development and enhancement of self-esteem for their sons/daughters and the parents are primary concerns.

The Yes-No Process (page 32) that you used with your students is an excellent activity to teach to your parents' support group. They will not only appreciate how the skills learned with those exercises will enable and protect their sons and daughters, they will be better equipped to support their children's growth towards independence.

The Body Tracing Activity (page 87) is also one that parents will enjoy and appreciate. Instead of lying down on the floor on a large piece of paper, invite them to draw an outline of themselves on an 8 ½" x 11" piece of paper. No one else has to see it.

OVERCOMING MYTHS REGARDING PHYSICALLY CHALLENGED INDIVIDUALS– FOR PARENTS

You as the counselor, group leader or teacher may need to clarify your own attitudes toward sexuality before working with others' attitudes. So, too, do parents have to clarify their own attitudes. Sex doesn't have to be a heavy subject. Sex is, after all, fun and feels good, so the lighter the mood, the better. Wouldn't it be wonderful if we could all sit around and talk about sex with the same ease and comfort we feel when we talk about movies or a football game?

Many parents view their physically challenged daughter or son as asexual or devoid of any sexual or sensual desires, much less as able to satisfy any of these desires in any way. No wonder those young people also view themselves as asexual. It serves no purpose to blame the parents, the son or daughter, or anyone. There is no blame. Instead, there is a situation that has great promise to be resolved, directly or indirectly. Parents need to become aware that there are people who are severely physically challenged (loss of sensation, movement, movement control, body parts) who still have satisfactory sexual, sensual and emotional interpersonal relationships, whether heterosexual, homosexual, autosexual or any combination. These relationships are satisfying not only to themselves, but also to their partners.

Myths are often cherished beliefs that at one time or other seemed to serve some useful purpose of explanation. Unfortunately these beliefs or myths may now be hindering the growth and maturation process of people with disabilities and of their parents as well. How can you change these myths, especially when they have been incorporated into a belief system that feels comfortable?

One way may be to compile a list of myths appropriate for discussion. These myths may also be useful for discussions with students. Here are some examples of prevailing myths pertaining to the physically challenged population:

1. Physically challenged young adults are too immature to integrate their feelings and desires effectively. Therefore, they are best off not getting involved at a sexual level.
2. Young people with cerebral palsy experience severely painful spasms with sexual activity. Therefore, sexual activity should be discouraged for their own good.
3. Physically challenged people are sexually exploited more often than non-challenged people.
4. Physically challenged persons are too dependent to have a satisfactory sex life.
5. Passive behavior is the only option available to the handicapped, both socially and sexually. Assertive behavior will be rejected.
6. Sexual energy should be channeled to more important purposes (schoolwork, physical therapy, hobbies, etc.).
7. Sexual responses are only for married couples to please the partner.
8. Spinal-cord injured people cannot experience sexual pleasure.
9. Spinal-cord injured people cannot provide sexual pleasure for any partner.
10. Spinal-cord injured people cannot sire or conceive offspring.
11. Physically challenged persons cannot make love normally, or in the right way, the way everybody else does.
12. Physically challenged people do not like to touch others or be touched.
13. Normal sensation must be present in the genitalia. Otherwise, no satisfying sexual experience may take place.
14. To maintain one's dignity in lovemaking, one must hold everything in (e.g. breathing, sounds, movements, excitement).
15. You are only as other people perceive you.

TEACHER-PARENT DISCUSSIONS IN PREPARATION FOR SEX EDUCATION
Divide parents into groups of three to discuss questions such as those below. Feel free to add your own or use the *Feeling Good Playful Question Cards*. Each person chooses three questions from the list that he or she feels comfortable discussing.
1. How did you first find out about sex?
2. How did you feel? What were your reactions when you found out?
3. Who was the most important sex educator in your life?
4. What sexual misconception affected your growing up most?
5. How did you first become aware of your own sexuality?
6. As you grew up, what were the general and specific attitudes about touching, holding, hugging and showing affection? At school? At work? At home?
7. How would you have liked to learn about sex if you had it to do again?
8. Is sex for everyone?
9. If you were a member of the opposite sex for one week, what experiences would you seek?
10. What makes you feel good?
11. If you could be a child for one week, what experiences would you seek?
12. Name three things you like best about your body.
13. How would you be different if you were perfect?

Winifred Kempton's outline of questions and answers for parents of students who have developmental disabilities is found in Appendix B.

CHECKLIST FOR FUTURE PARENTS' MEETINGS
I would like to learn more about:
1. Self-esteem.
2. Teaching appropriate behavior.
3. Teaching my teenage son/daughter to see himself or herself as a young adult.
4. Fostering independence in my son/daughter.
5. Encouraging assertiveness in my son/daughter.
6. How to discuss honestly:
    a. Body and emotional changes and needs during teen years.
    b. Dating.
    c. Marriage.
    d. Parenting.
    e. How babies are made.
    f. Sexual readiness.
    g. Birth control.
    h. STD.
7. How to avoid situations that might lead to rape or victimization.
8. Legal rights and resources for people who have developmental disabilities.
9. Is there anything else you would like to add?

PRELIMINARY INVENTORY OF PERSONAL, SOCIAL AND SEXUAL EXPERIENCES AND ATTITUDES

The following are specific objectives for learning:
1. To gain understanding about the social and sexual experience/sophistication of the group.
2. To learn the educational needs of the class in the areas of socialization and sex information.

Maturity level: age 13+

This is a useful preliminary activity for the teacher or group leader to gain some understanding of what experience and knowledge the group may already have had in terms of sexuality and self-concept. It is not necessary if the teacher is already familiar with persons in the group. It never hurts, however, to take an inventory of experience first, as appearances can often be deceiving. You cannot always assume that someone else means exactly what you think their statement means. For example, "Oh, yes, we made love...," translated later may mean, "We kissed." You and your class can watch your "head" and "gut" in response to these topics. It is entirely normal for your "gut" to respond one way and your "head" another. For any of these discussions you may choose to separate the male and female group members or keep them together.

The checklist method is useful with nonreaders as it requires only "yes" or "no" responses (symbolic or written). Embarrassment is prevented by anonymous responses. Materials are a chalk-board, small pieces of paper and pencils.

The leader gives each student a piece of paper and instructs the group to put a number one on all the papers given out for the first question, put number two on all the papers given out for the second question, etc. Then ask each question (below). Each person writes "yes" or "no" (or makes a mark in red or blue, or circle or X, on the paper for that question. Ask the next question and mark answer on next piece of paper. Collect papers after each question and put them into a hat. Discuss each question and count up "yes" and "no" responses. Group members can then see that they are not alone. Tally answers on the chalkboard. Ask your group, "How did you experience yourself responding to these questions? What was your "head" response? Your "gut" response?"

Questions for response and discussion:
1. Have you ever felt pretty/handsome?
2. Have you ever felt ugly?
3. Have you ever telephoned someone of the opposite sex? (a peer)
4. Have you ever felt rejected by someone of the opposite sex? (Explain "rejected" simply and briefly.)
5. Have you ever been on a date?
6. Have you ever kissed someone of the opposite sex on the lips? (a peer)
7. Have you ever felt horny? (explain "horny" briefly and simply)
8. Have you ever "petted" or been petted by someone of the opposite sex? (explain)
9. Have you ever masturbated? (When you explain this word, it's important that you communicate that this practice, done in a private place, is normal and natural.)
10. Have you ever been seen nude by someone of the same sex? (peer group, not to include a doctor, nurse or parent)
11. Have you ever seen someone else of the same sex nude? (also a peer)
12. Have you ever seen someone of the opposite sex nude?
13. Have you ever been seen by someone of the opposite sex nude?

14. Have you ever had sexual intercourse? (You will most likely have to show a drawing of a man and woman having sexual intercourse and asking, "Have you done this?")
15. Do you know what a climax (or orgasm) is?
16. Have you ever had an orgasm?
17. Have you ever been pregnant or gotten someone pregnant?
18. Have you ever had an abortion, or had a close friend whom you helped when she was having an abortion?

Some of these questions may be inappropriate for your particular group, or certain additional questions might be useful for you to ask. The important thing to remember here is that no judgment is implied here. You are only gathering information for yourself and for the group members to get a general idea of how knowledgeable or experienced they may be in certain broad areas of sexual behavior.

Alternative and additional preliminary activities:
1. List on the board the following subjects:

Male Sex System	Reproduction	Making Out
Female Sex System	Birth Control	Petting
Masturbation	Homosexual Behavior	Sexual Intercourse
Wet Dreams	Slang Terms	Being Masculine
STD (Sexually Transmitted Disease)		Being Feminine
		Menstruation

2. Ask students, "Which would you like to know more about and discuss?" Put numbers before each topic indicating the topics of most interest to the class.
3. Ask students, "Which subjects would you *not* like to know about or discuss?" Put numbers after each topic indicating their negative importance. (These are probably the things we would grow most from discussing and which we need most to talk about with each other.)
4. Provide a box in the room for questions and encourage the students to put unsigned questions into the box for the week preceding this discussion.

GETTING TO KNOW ONE'S BODY
SEXUAL SELF-AWARENESS

Maturity level: **age 13+**

The following are specific objectives for learning:
1. To gain awareness of one's own body and body history including disabilities.
2. To become familiar with conventional and slang vocabulary for sexual anatomy.
3. To gain understanding of the male anatomy and how it works.
4. To gain understanding of the female anatomy and how it works.
5. To become aware of similarities and differences in male and female anatomy.
6. To understand the normal physical changes during puberty in males and females.
7. To understand the process of menstruation.
8. To express feelings associated with bodily and emotional changes occurring during puberty.

PHYSICAL DEVELOPMENT FROM CHILDHOOD TO ADULTHOOD

Materials: Charts showing nude male and female physical development from baby, to child, to adolescent, to adult. Photos (clothed) of leader and students at different ages.

1. Ask class to place each photo of themselves alongside the body chart that matches the age they were in each photo.
2. Review their physical development shown in the chart with the corresponding photos of themselves.
3. Say, "If you are a male or a man, raise your hand."
4. Say, "If you are a female or a woman, raise your hand."
5. Explain that when people grow from being children into becoming men or becoming women, this is called puberty. Ask everyone to repeat the word, puberty.
6. Using the male and female physical development charts, brainstorm with the class and list the changes that take place from childhood to adulthood during puberty. Ex: axillary hair, pubic hair, facial hair, breasts, acne, voice changes, height changes, shape changes.
7. Discuss that everyone goes through puberty at different ages, different times. Men change in ways similar to all other men, and women change in ways similar to all other women. Whenever and however your body changes, it's normal for your body.
8. Place male and female physical development charts where everyone can see them. Ask every person: "Point to the picture that looks like your body and then say, 'I am a woman/I am a man'." This gives the teacher insight into the students' physical self-concept. *I was amazed to find out that my 67-year-old male client saw his own body as that of a 12-year-old boy when he pointed to the chart.*
9. Say, "Everyone was once a baby and everyone changes at different rates at different times." Discuss the physical differences within the room. Assure them that differences are normal and that everyone is to a certain extent different, just as everyone is to a certain extent the same.
10. Say, "Now that you are young men and women, your bodies can do things that you could not do when you were children." List these things:
    a. Women have periods each month.
    b. Men may have wet dreams (explain).
    c. Men and women sometimes experience strong sexual feelings. We'll learn more about that later.
    d. Women can become mothers. Men can become fathers.
    e. Men and women become physically stronger.

Activity: Body Tracing

This is usually done on large pieces of paper. One person lies down flat on paper while a partner traces around the other's body with pencil or crayon.

1. Choose and draw with one color, any operations, scars, bruises, scrapes, old or new, on your body. Use cross-hatching (###).
2. Using another color, draw any tightness, aches, pains (headaches, menstrual cramps, backaches) or worries on the drawing. Use jagged lines (∿).
3. Choose another color to show the favorite parts of your body. Use circles.
4. Use another color to indicate the parts of your body you might want to change, and how.
5. Draw **X**'s where you do not like to be touched.
6. Draw hearts where you do like to be touched.
7. Hang the drawings up in the room at each person's level of height when drawings are complete.
8. Each person shares 1 through 6 and what their disabilities include.

THE MALE SEXUAL SYSTEM

External sex organs are not usually altered in individuals with disabilities.

Brainstorm the names for the male genitalia and write the names on the board including scientific terms, family terminology and slang. Use anatomy charts and body tracings to locate these parts.

It is preferable if these lessons can be led by a male teacher and the lessons about the female sexual system to be led by a woman, especially for the discussions about sexual details, ejaculation, menstruation, hygiene, etc.

1. External sex organs:
    a. Penis (cock, dick, prick, weenie, peter, thing, rod, wang, pecker).
    b. Glans penis (tip).
    c. Urethra.
    d. Foreskin (absent if circumcised).
    e. Scrotum (sack, bag).
    f. Testes (testicles, balls, nuts, rocks).
2. Internal sex organs are:
    a. Prostate gland
    b. Epididymis
    c. Vas deferens
    d. Seminal vesicles

Note: for less sophisticated groups, 2. Internal sex organs: b, c and d (and even a) may not be relevant to the discussion.

Puberty is an opportune time to affirm to teens a new beginning in their lives. The males are blossoming into handsome, strong, responsible and more independent adult men and the females are blossoming into beautiful, more responsible and more independent adult women. Discuss in affirming details how their bodies, self-concepts, expectations and responsibilities change in adulthood.

PUBERTY: MALE PHYSICAL CHANGES

Puberty and adolescence are often prolonged in disabled individuals. It takes dependent people longer to gain sexual identity. Reassure the late-bloomers that it is normal for some people to take longer to develop adult characteristics. Point out that it's not unusual to feel left out or embarrassed until their hormones kick in.

1. When? In males, usually between ages 13 and 18 but can be earlier or later.
2. What happens? Male sex hormone (testosterone) production increases to cause the following changes:
    a. Primary sexual characteristics (occurring simultaneously):
        (1. Penis, testicles, prostate and seminal vesicles enlarge and mature.
        (2. Testicles begin to produce sperm.
    b. Secondary sexual characteristics (may occur gradually):
        (1. Appearance of facial, axillary, pubic and body hair; possibly a change in hairline later on.
        (2. Acne.
        (3. Voice deepens.
        (4. Change in body configuration with bone and muscle growth spurt followed later by completion of bone growth (no further increase in height).
        (5. Increased libido, increased frequency of erections (Note: spastic people have normal erections), start experiencing feeling "horny." The male students form a group to discuss and share the changes and

feelings they have/are experiencing, while the women share their feelings in their own group. Use your discretion as to the readiness of the class for coed sharing.

    a. Erection (hard-on, boner, woody):
        i. What causes it to happen? Physical stimulation, mental stimulation, intentional and unintentional. Persons with spinal cord lesions and no penil sensation may be able to utilize mental stimulation to obtain erection.
        ii. How does it happen? Blood flow out of the penis is restricted, causing engorgement of the blood vessels within the penis.
    b. Ejaculation (coming):
        i. What is it? (The expulsion of semen that accompanies orgasm. It is not urine.)
        ii. What is in it? (In the adult, fertile male, there are sperm in the ejaculatory fluid. Sperm cells from a man can fertilize the egg cells in a woman to create a baby. There may be no sperm in the fluid in pre and early pubescent males nor in men with vasectomies.) Young boys may experience the muscular sensations of ejaculation during orgasm with no discharge of fluid.
    c. Seminal emission (wet dream, nocturnal emission):
        i. What is it? Involuntary non-intentional release of seminal fluid. **This is a perfectly normal, natural phenomenon not necessitating feelings of guilt.**
        ii When? During erotic dreams that culminate with ejaculation.
        iii How? Psychological stimulation (fantasy), or from physical stimulation by sheets or bed clothes rubbing and causing stimulation.
        iv Point out that if this occurs, the individual should clean themselves off with a washcloth or towel and if necessary put their sheets in the laundry hamper.

6. Discuss genital cleanliness (the circumcised and uncircumcised penis).

THE FEMALE SEXUAL SYSTEM

Brainstorm the different scientific, family terminology and slang words for female genitalia. Use anatomy charts and body tracings.

1. External primary sex organs are:
   a. Mons veneris.
   b. Vulva (box, cunt, pussy, snatch, crack, twat, beaver). Note: each female looks a little different. That's normal.
   c. Labia majora (outer lips).
   d. Labia minora (inner lips).
   e. Hymen (cherry, maidenhead).
   f. Clitoris (clit, button).
   g. Urethra.
   h. Bartholin's glands (not usually visible).

2. Internal primary sex organs are:
    a. Vagina (hole).
    b. Uterus, cervix.
    c. Fallopian tubes.
    d. Ovaries.
3. Secondary sex organs:
    Breasts, nipples (boobs, tits, titties, bazooms, knockers).

PUBERTY: FEMALE PHYSICAL CHANGES
   Maturity level: age 11+
1. When? (In females puberty is marked by the onset of menstruation, commonly between ages 10 to 14, sometimes occurring earlier or later.)
2. What happens? Female sex hormone production increases (estrogen and progesterone) causing the following changes:
    a. Axillary hair develops, pubic hair appears
    b. Breasts develop, hips get wider, body contours rounded.
    c. Uterus enlarges
    d. Bone growth (with increase in height) begins to slow down and then stop. Because girls usually reach puberty before boys do, they stop growing in height earlier as well.
    e. There is also increase in testosterone level (male sex hormone) in pubertal females which causes:
        (1. Acne
        (2. Increased libido (more interest in sex).
3. Menstruation (If a student has a physical disability affecting the central nervous system, especially the pituitary gland, menstruation may be affected.)

Remember the story about the young teenager (on page 31) who was a slow learner. She had just started menstruating. No one had informed her that all women have periods and she interpreted her monthly bleeding and physical changes as punishment. She thought she was going to die from the bleeding. She buried her soiled underwear fearful of being found out as being different than other people. If this young woman had an informed, askable friend or relative she could consult without fear, she could have enjoyed the feelings and knowledge of becoming a woman, becoming an adult like other people she looked up to. She could have had a new self-concept to build upon by knowing that she had more in common with the rest of the human species. Wouldn't it have made a difference if she had someone who taught her what to expect from her normal development? They could have used this opportunity to affirm a new beginning and bonding with other women. "How wonderful! You are becoming a woman. You are blossoming into a beautiful more independent woman!" From this foundation of commonality, she (and all of us) can build healthy and enabling self-concepts. We build on what we have in common, as well as our individual uniquenesses, and then we share experiences of success.

   a. Use an anatomy chart or illustration to describe the process of menstruation. Information describing the process and cycle of ovulation is available in most health textbooks.
   b. Menstrual discharge: What is it? How much?

(1. Blood.
(2. mucus and endometrial tissue.
(3. approximately two ounces during the period.
c. Cycles of onset of period range from 26 to 34 days (range may vary)
(1. may be irregular until 18 to 20 years of age.
(2. irregularities after age 20 may be related to emotional stress.
d. Duration of period (discharge) usually lasts from 3 to 7 days (longer may indicate an abnormal condition or a problem.)
e. Some women experience the following symptoms:
(1. menstrual pains related to uterine spasms (cramps); cramps usually decrease after childbirth.
(2. migraine-type headaches.
(3. weight gain due to retention of fluids or increased appetite, swollen ankles.
(4. Emotional lability, mood swings, irritability.
f. What does one do with discharge?
(1. Show samples of pads, tampons, etc.
(2. How does one use and properly place each? Discuss how to dispose of sanitary supplies.
(a. The women may want to form their own group(s) to share techniques they may have discovered to work.
(b. The women may want to share feelings, attitudes and experiences before, during and related to their periods.
(c. Discuss genital cleanliness.

Activity: Getting to Know Your Body (a personal activity)
Maturity level: 16+
Suggest that each student, particularly the young women, spend some time alone looking at their own genitals with a hand mirror in the privacy of the bedroom or bathroom with the door shut. When the female students meet again, allow for discussion and processing of their reactions to this experience of themselves.

MALE AND FEMALE COMPARISONS

Anatomy illustrations:
1. Reproductive Anatomy Charts (see Resources)*
2. Illustrations showing similarities of external male and female genitalia (development from undifferentiated into differentiated stage).*

Review similarities between male and female changes of puberty:
1. Voice changes.
2. Height.
3. More curves and muscle development.
4. Axillary and pubic hair.
5. Need to wash more often and use deodorant.
6. Acne (bumps), need to wash face more often.
7. Increased emotional sensitivity.

---

* Reproductive Anatomy Charts, Planned Parenthood, MN.
* Atlas of Human Anatomy, Frank Netter, MD

8. Increased genital sensitivity (It's OK to touch oneself in these areas in private when you are alone because it feels good. It's also OK not to touch private body parts).

Review differences between male and female changes of puberty:

Men	Women
Men's physical shape changes.	Women's physical shape changes.
They develop larger muscles.	Their pelvis gets wider.
Shoulders may get wider.	Breasts enlarge.
Men develop facial and chest hair (some men have less hair than others - that's normal).	Women do not develop facial hair (or much less hair than men).
Men start puberty later than women.	Women start puberty earlier than men.
Men may start having wet dreams	Women begin to menstruate.
Men can impregnate women.	Women can have babies.

SEXUAL ACTIVITY

MASTURBATION

Maturity level: age 12+

The following are specific objectives for learning:
1. To clarify what masturbation is.
2. To understand that masturbation is normal, pleasurable, an accepted method of achieving sexual satisfaction.
3. To become aware of appropriate and inappropriate times and places to masturbate.
4. To become aware of the myths that affect our emotions and attitudes toward masturbation and ourselves.
5. To become aware of erogenous zones.
6. To become aware of the role of erotic fantasies in sexuality.
7. To become aware of devices available for masturbation.
8. To become aware of masturbation as natural and okay with a partner.
9. To become aware of how an individual's disability relates to masturbation and orgasm.

Activity: Group Discussion
Maturity level: 12+
1. Ask your group, "What is masturbation?" *The leader can thus get an idea about the sophistication of the group and what they know, what they don't know, and what may confuse them.*
2. Brainstorm different slang words for masturbation (whacking off, jerking off, diddling, etc.).
3. Definition:
   "Masturbation is the act of rhythmically rubbing or stroking the penis or pressing the genital area or stimulating the clitoris with the fingers. Either sex may also masturbate with friction against objects. This stimulation produces pleasure and with sufficient activity may lead to orgasm. Masturbation is more frequently enjoyed alone but may also be a mutual experience." (Calderwood)

The act of giving oneself sexual pleasure, arousal or excitement through touching parts of one's body is called masturbation; a way of smiling to ourselves, taking time to be good to ourselves in a natural way. Only you can really know what is "natural" and exciting for you by experimenting and experiencing this playful pleasure in an infinite number of ways. It is the most personal way you can use your imagination. By knowing how to give yourself pleasure, you will also know how to teach or show your partner how and where you enjoy being stimulated.

According to Betty Dodson, Ph.D. in her book *Sex for One,* "Seeking sexual satisfaction is a basic drive and masturbation is our first natural sexual activity. It's the way we discover our eroticism, the way we learn to respond sexually, a way we learn to love ourselves and build self-esteem. Sexual skill and the ability to respond are not 'natural' in our society. Doing what 'comes naturally' for us is to be sexually inhibited. Sex is like any other skill, it has to be learned and practiced. When a woman or man masturbates, she/he learns to like her/his own genitals, to enjoy sex and orgasm and furthermore to become proficient and independent about it. Our society is made uncomfortable by sexually proficient and independent individuals."

Many of us experience this discomfort by feeling guilty and fearful of "being found out" by adults who don't understand. They too, may not have recognized their own rights as sexual human beings; they too were influenced by parents, peers and clergy who felt that masturbation was bad and caused all kinds of catastrophic consequences. If masturbation brings on overwhelming feelings of guilt and anxiety, then it is important that they discuss their beliefs, concerns and misinformation with someone who is informed, comfortable and non-judgmental on this topic.

If an individual, especially an institutionalized person, does nothing else but masturbate, it may be because there is nothing else more stimulating to do in that setting. The client, out of boredom, finds their own stimulation. When institutionalized residents spend too much time masturbating it indicates that the daily program is inadequate.

MYTHS THAT CAUSE CONFLICT:

***Maturity level*: select the myths that are appropriate for your group to discuss.**
1. Masturbation will cause hair or warts to grow on your palms.
2. God will punish anyone who touches oneself "down below."
3. If you masturbate, you will lose the energy needed to accomplish anything.
4. Masturbation is unhealthy, unnatural; and what kind of person would even want to do it?
5. People who masturbate are more likely to become sex criminals.
6. People who masturbate cannot achieve orgasm with a partner.
7. Masturbation will threaten sexual relationships. No one will respect you or want to be with you if they know.
8. Masturbation causes: "insanity; epilepsy; headaches; eye disease; intermittent deafness; redness of nose, nose bleeds; hallucinations of smell and hearing; hypertrophy; tenderness in the breasts; afflictions of the ovaries, uterus and vagina, including painful menstruation and 'acidity of the vagina'; asthma; heart murmurs ('Masturbator's heart'); skin ailments ranging from acne to warts; pale and discolored skin; and 'an undesirable odor of the skin of women.' " (Note: None of this is true. There is no evidence to support claims of mental or physical harm caused by masturbation.)
9. Masturbation stunts your growth.
10. Masturbation is bad for sports.

11. Masturbation causes mental retardation.
12. Masturbation causes problems when you marry.
13. People can tell if you masturbate.
14. People who masturbate are perverted sexually.
15. Masturbation is a sign of immaturity.
16. People only masturbate when they are "hard up."
17. If a woman masturbates, she is no longer a virgin.
18. A male who masturbates frequently need not worry about birth control.
19. Orgasm from masturbating is inferior to orgasm achieved during sexual intercourse.
20. If a woman masturbates a man with hand or mouth, she can become pregnant.

Activity: Questions for a discussion session:
1. What myths do or have you believed?
2. When is it appropriate to masturbate?
3. When is it not appropriate to masturbate?
4. How do men masturbate?
5. Why do men masturbate?
6. How do women masturbate?
7. Why do women masturbate?
8. Do married people masturbate?
9. What happens when men masturbate?
10. Is it okay not to masturbate?
11. Is it true that "whacking off" is an expression for masturbation?
12. Is it true that women who masturbate more likely know what makes them feel good sexually?
13. Is it true that men who masturbate more likely know what makes them feel good sexually?

SHARING MASTURBATION

Maturity level: adult
Any couple whether disabled or not, may find this as a natural, convenient, pleasurable and practical method of sexual play. Adaptive devices (vibrators, etc.) may also be available for shared usage.

The role of staff personnel in any hospital or other domiciliary residence as masturbation facilitators is a question that merits consideration. The answer is that in nearly every situation it will not be appropriate. In rare circumstances, with individuals who are markedly disabled and who have unique problems (some are described below), there may be such a role. Any such decisions must first be considered and approved by the highest authorities in the facility as well as with the explicit permission of that client and his or her parents.

ADAPTIVE DEVICES

Maturity level: adult
1. Dildos, rubber or plastic artificial penises.
    A situation arose in a foster home where a female resident was inserting sharp objects into her anus. She was medically evaluated to be sure there was no lesion or infection that might, for example, have been causing itching. We learned that she was using these objects to masturbate. Because these sharp objects were potentially dangerous, she was given a safer device, a dildo, to use instead. She was shown a video so that she could see how it could be used with

lubrication and how it should be cleaned. The video showed her that the dildo could be used in her vagina. She was taught how to use it in a private place and the problem was successfully resolved.

2. Vibrators.
    a. Massager vibrators
    b. Penis shaped vibrators
    c. Vagina shaped vibrators and other male masturbation devices have been used in institutions for physically handicapped as well as mentally retarded males who either don't have the physical ability or the attention span to complete the task.
    We were told about a mentally retarded man with a short attention span, who, when he become frustrated while masturbating, would hit and slap his penis. The device helped him to resolve that problem.
    These devices may be available in adult sex shops or in the Internet. One of the first of these devices ("AcuJack") had hygiene problems. Newer designs claim to have eliminated that problem.
    d. Whirlpool bath, aerating nozzles, portable showerhead.
4. Lubricants.

EROGENOUS ZONES

Maturity level: age 12+

These are areas of the body that are especially sensitive and responsive to sexual stimulation. In fact, every part of your body is capable of feeling stimulated. The most commonly recognized areas include:

1. Clitoris.
2. Vagina, including surrounding skin, inner and outer lips, and inside.
3. Penis (the undersurface is generally more sensitive as well as the tip).
4. Scrotum.
5. Breasts and nipples (female *and* male).
6. Body orifices (mouth, ears, anus, etc.).
7. Skin folds (armpits, neck, between fingers and toes, etc.).
8. Everywhere and anywhere else where you feel good being touched.

This is especially important to keep in mind when working with people who are physically disabled. Persons with spinal cord injuries may at first feel that they have been deprived of the availability of some of their erogenous zones. For instance, anesthesia below the waist (or even below the neck) may at first appear to rule out enjoyment of sexual stimulation of the genitals and therefore a loss of sexual ability. But this is not correct. When such persons have the interest and encouragement to explore their own body, they may discover several delightful surprises. The sensations perceived in the transition areas between normal and anesthetic skin may be zones of eroticism. Also, even with seeming complete injury to the upper spinal cord, sensation to the sacral area, especially around the rectum, may be preserved.

Altered sensation to the genitalia in a man may still permit erection from psychological stimulation without the normal tactile sensibility. He may be able to prolong his erection for as long as he desires. This may make him even more attractive to a partner and he may still enjoy his experience as much as before, if not more so, but in a different way.

With total anesthesia of the lower half of the body, the upper half may become erotically active. Stroking the neck can bring a delightful climax. We can learn much from that supposedly "handicapped" person. If he can climax from having his neck rubbed, possibly so can anyone else! (See Orgasm, below.) And how about the eyes and the mouth that can lovingly communicate the most wonderful eroticism. Most important of all, **giving** as well as receiving sexual and sensual pleasure to a partner can be exciting and satisfying to both people. The most powerful sex organ rests between one's shoulders: the brain.

There are classical erogenous zones and traditional experience limits them to a few special parts of the body. But those erogenous zones are not the only part of the body that feel good and respond when stroked. Have you ever had a good foot massage? It is a real pleasure. It may not be "erotic" which may mean that it's okay to receive a foot massage from someone with whom you are not intimate. But if a couple wishes it to be erotic, who is to deny having that experience? It is important to be careful not to deny the sexual experience, or the sexuality of an experience, to some individual with disability out of one's own inexperience, ignorance or discomfort. Exploration is the key to eroticism.

ORGASM

Maturity level: **age 16+**

What is an orgasm? With sexual stimulation the individual experiences a gradual build-up of tension in their body. This may be experienced as a stronger pulse, more rapid pulse, more blood to head (blushing), more rapid breathing and muscular tension. There may be changes in attention and consciousness of the immediate environment. This tension increases to a certain level until there is an intensely pleasurable release that is often somewhat sudden, sometimes seemingly explosive. There may be particular sensations of rhythmic muscular contractions within the pelvis and in other parts of the body. After the release there is usually a feeling of well being, relaxation or relief. Pulse and respiration may rapidly decrease to normal. Ejaculation in a man is not necessarily the same as an orgasm. The two phenomena, though usually linked, can be separate physiologic events.

At a conference on sexuality and disability, a quadriplegic man, paralyzed and anesthetic from the neck down resulting from a spinal cord injury at age 17, described how he could become sexually stimulated by stroking his neck until he became thoroughly aroused to the point of orgasm. He experienced this throughout his body as a build-up of erotic tension that climaxed with a pleasurable release despite the complete absence of all genital sensation and without ejaculation. If this so-called handicapped man can achieve orgasm by stroking his neck, think what possibilities this presents to persons with unrestricted sensations in all parts of their bodies!

Note to the teacher or leader. The following topics may cause your class or you some concern or anxiety. Nevertheless, these activities are appropriate for discussion. Groups vary in their sophistication. You may wish to remind your group: "You don't have to do, or have done to you, anything you don't want." Review saying, "No. I don't like that, but I do like…"

EROTIC FANTASIES

Maturity level: **age 16+**

Any thought, any visual or auditory image that causes sexual arousal, can be classified as an erotic fantasy. Many individuals enjoy masturbating while they fantasize, read an erotic book or look at erotic art or pornography. They let their imaginations go. It is important that we communicate that fantasizing is *normal* and not to be feared. How many of us have had erotic fantasies? There's no need for guilt about erotic fantasies or masturbation. By themselves thoughts or fantasies are not harmful. Inappropriate behavior can be harmful. Thoughts or fantasies do not automatically lead to actions. There's a big difference. Most people have fantasies, even ones that they would never want to actually occur. Most people do not act them out. They remain just as thoughts.

Activity: Discussion/Sharing
1. Ask class members to report on popular songs, movies, advertisements, books, comics, music, etc. that might be sexually stimulating. These may be sought from the common, ordinary, everyday media; not necessarily limited to X-rated events.
2. Have each member of class choose a same-sex partner with whom he or she would be comfortable sharing a sexual fantasy. If people are willing to share their feelings of discomfort about sharing fantasies, this too can be a valuable exchange. How do you feel when you think of sharing a sexual fantasy? **Honor people's limits.**

ORAL SEX

Activity: Discussion
Maturity level: adult
1. Definition: An individual (male or female) uses their mouth or tongue on another's genitalia (male or female) and/or anus.
2. Brainstorm different words for oral sex (scientific and slang). Ex: fellatio, cunnilingus, going down, blow-job, eating out, licking, sucking, sucking off, giving head, kissing down there, rimming, sixty-nine.
3. Stress that no one should be forced or manipulated to perform oral sex.
4. Oral sex has no risk of pregnancy but it does carry the risk of disease transmission. Oral sex with anyone other than a long-term trustworthy partner in a monogamous relationship is unsafe unless the male is wearing a condom. A woman with STD or who is menstruating is also not a safe sex partner.

SAFE SEX

Maturity level: age 14+
Safe sex generally refers to sexual activity where there is no risk of transmitting disease nor of causing pregnancy.

1. Solitary masturbation is obviously a safe sex practice.
2. Two individuals who masturbate themselves in the presence of each other is another form of safe sex. Mutual masturbation is usually a safe sex practice.
3. Certain diseases such as hepatitis and HIV which can be transmitted by blood or semen can be passed from one person to another during oral sex.
4. If during mutual masturbation the blood of one infected individual (such as menstrual fluid) or the semen of one infected individual were to come in contact with an open wound on the partner (for instance if the partner had a cut on his or her hand) there is the theoretical risk of disease transmission but this is extremely unlikely.
5. AIDS is not transmitted by kissing (mouth to mouth). Kissing is safe sex.
6. Unprotected oral sex where the menstrual blood or the ejaculate from one person can enter the mouth of the partner can lead to disease transmission.

7. Unprotected sexual intercourse (meaning that the male is not wearing a rubber condom) whether vaginal or anal can lead to disease transmission.
8. Protected sex with a rubber condom used properly is safe sex if the condom doesn't break.
9. Sex is safe if both partners know each other, both are honest with each other, both are monogamous (with each other) and have been so for many years, and/or both have had tests for STD including hepatitis and AIDS done in a timely fashion.

PHYSICAL DISABILITIES AFFECTING SEXUAL FUNCTION

Maturity level: adult
1. Spinal cord injury, flaccid paralysis
    a. Male
        (1. Usually no erections.
        (2. No genital orgasm.
    b. Female
        (1. No clitoral erection.
        (2. No genital orgasm.
2. Spinal cord injury, spastic paralysis
    a. Male
        (1. Erogenous areas may be above level of lesion (the neck may be especially erotically sensitive, also the anus).
        (2. Reflex erection from psychological stimuli or fantasy without genital stimulation.
        (3. No genital orgasm.
        (4. Infrequent ejaculation (may pass urine).
        (5. May develop hypertension, perspiration, headache.
    b. Female
        (1. Irregular sensation.
        (2. May develop muscular spasm.
        (3. Other responses / reactions similar to males.
3. Spina bifida (myelo-meningocele)
    a. Male
        (1. Erections infrequent and varied.
        (2. Psychogenic and reflex stimulation may be possible.
        (3. Genital orgasm infrequent.
        (4. Ejaculation infrequent.
    b. Female
        (1. Sensation usually absent.
        (2. Genital orgasm infrequent.
4. Cerebral palsy
    a. Male and Female
        (1. Sensation and erection may be normal or nearly so.
        (2. Sexual stimulation may cause agitation.
        (3. Hyperactive reflexes make stimulation awkward.
        (4. Orgasm possible.
        (5. Premature ejaculation common.
5. Muscular dystrophy: reduced strength and stamina may be present.
6. Multiple sclerosis
    a. Any and all of the above conditions including altered sensation and/or spasticity may be present.

      b. Conditions improve at times and then regress.
      c. Pregnancy extremely deleterious.
      d. Psychological problems are common.

The preceding disabilities also share these potential problems:
1. Masturbation may be awkward or impossible if there is severe motor incoordination. *A partner who is not handicapped, less handicapped or differently handicapped can be helpful.*
2. A urinary catheter can cause difficulty with sexual intercourse.
3. Sudden muscular spasms and/or joint contractions may make positions difficult.

ERECTILE DYSFUNCTION

If the male with a physical disability has difficulty obtaining or maintaining an erection, medication is now available that may overcome this problem. That client's physician best decides whether or not the medication is indicated.

Depending on which partner is handicapped in what way, satisfaction may still be attained with patience and experimentation.

SEXUAL INTERCOURSE

Maturity level: age 13+

The group or class leader cannot take for granted that anyone in the group knows exactly what is meant by "sexual intercourse." The slang words, fucking, screwing, making love, going all the way, or making it, are often misinterpreted. When I have asked, "Raise your hand if you have ever made love," nearly everyone in the room raised their hand with great excitement. Upon further questioning I found out that their definitions of sexual intercourse included everything from holding hands to kissing on a full moon to an excited male's ejaculation inside his clothing while dancing close to his girlfriend.

I have used a drawing or a magazine photo of a couple having sexual intercourse. I showed the image to the individuals and asked them, "Is this what you did?" Not infrequently the response was a blushing statement like: "Oh no! Ick! We just touched each other down there."

"Sexual intercourse" is the act of penetrating the woman's vagina with the man's penis. That's the way virginity is lost and that's the only way (except for artificial insemination) that a woman can become pregnant. As for the inevitable questions about toilet seats, swimming pools and heavy petting, it is probably technically possible for a few sperm to survive for a short time in some alternate environment and then for them to drift into a passing vagina where they could then enter the cervix and travel the necessary path to reach and then fertilize a waiting ovum. But the likelihood of that complex series of events ever happening is not great enough to even consider.

Sometime in the course of your sexuality program you will most likely have to present this clear and precise definition to avoid future misunderstandings. The photographs from a pornographic magazine showing couples engaged in sexual intercourse (as well as fellatio and cunnilingus) can clarify many questions very simply and explicitly. We prefer sketches however, because they are less emotionally charged.

Sexual intercourse is also far more than a physical act described in a pornographic magazine or even in a medical journal and it is more than a clinical process used to make babies or a way of passing on disease. It is meant to be an expression of love, affection, pleasure and connectedness between two adults who love each other. It is the consummation of marriage, it is the subject of poets, it is one of the greatest and most sublime experiences that two people who care most deeply for each other can experience. In this Guide we focus on the potential problems that can result from inappropriate sexual activity because there is rarely any need to promote sexual activity in the populations served by readers of this Guide. This does not mean that our intention is to frown upon the healthy expression of sexual activity in the appropriate settings.

HOW TO TEACH WHAT SEXUAL INTERCOURSE IS TO INDIVIDUALS WHO ARE MENTALLY RETARDED

Some parents and communities are uncomfortable using explicit photographs or rubber models of genitalia or even drawings. We have found that when parents know that this information helps to prevent sexual victimization, they are more likely to accept this educational process for their sons and daughters. If their son or daughter doesn't know what sexual intercourse is, they won't know what's happening to them when it happens (perhaps against their will) or what to do about it. They can be easily and repeatedly sexually victimized.

Activity: Group Discussion

1. Introduce the activity by asking the group the leading question: "Does anyone know how a man and a woman make a baby?" What is that called? Brainstorm (accept all slang words: fucking, coitus, intercourse, having sex, banging, making love, screwing, etc.). Explain that certain words that might be used with close friends of the same sex are not appropriate to use in other circumstances (in school, in public, with families, with members of the opposite sex).
2. Review body parts on the male and the female. Use the charts, drawings or rubber models of genitalia (including anus). The problem with rubber models is that they are isolated from the rest of the body. When people who are slow learners see an isolated piece of anatomy, they may not be able to generalize that it is part of the human body. This lesson will have to be repeated enough times in a variety of ways until the teacher is satisfied that the students do understand the concepts.
3. The penis has to be erect in order to penetrate the vagina. What is an erection? What causes an erection?
4. You must realize that teaching this topic can be awkward, even for "the experts." All parents face concerns and even major difficulty teaching sexuality to their children who are not disabled. A teacher in a classroom or an institution may have even more fears and challenges.

    I well recall teaching the mechanics of sexual intercourse and how babies are made in a classroom of young adults with developmental disabilities in San Francisco. I was using rubber models to show how an erect penis entered a vagina. As I pulled the penis out of the vagina, the rubber vagina came inside out causing all of us in the classroom to gasp with horror. Just then, the principal happened to walk into my classroom. I felt so embarrassed that I burst out laughing. So did the principal and everyone else in the class quickly joined in. My advice is, when in doubt, laugh.
5. A student might ask, "Why would anyone want to put a penis into a vagina? It's so yucky." This is a good topic for group discussion. It can also help the teacher appreciate the class' level of maturity on this subject.

Note: *In the context of this Guide, the parents of individuals who are physically/ intellectually/emotionally challenged may fear or resist any discussion of sexual intercourse. Sexual intercourse can lead not only to unwanted pregnancy but also to disease or death. It is feared because it can be an act of exploitation. Yet we must not forget that sexual intercourse between two loving consenting individuals can also lead to enormous pleasure and satisfaction. We always hope that the sexual partners will also be committed to one another's well being and that they will be responsible, loving, appropriate and respectful. We also know couples who are non-disabled can and do have sexual intercourse for all the wrong reasons all too often. Many of the parents as well as the teachers involved with these programs may have had unsatisfactory sexual experiences in their lives. But they may also have had pleasurable and meaningful sexual experiences in their lives, even when all the requirements for the perfect situation were not met each time.*

RESPONSIBILITIES OF THE SEX EDUCATOR

It's reasonable to assume that most of us received little or no valid information about sex before we began our sexual lives. It's almost certain that few of us received any accurate instruction about sexual intercourse before our first experience. Therefore, what is our responsibility in this respect as sex educators for individuals who are physically/intellectually/emotionally challenged individuals?

1. We do need to explain to our clients the mechanics of sexual intercourse if only to help prevent their victimization.
2. We do need to explain the consequences of sexual intercourse as part of educating our clients about the responsibilities of adulthood and adult behavior. Pregnancy, STD prevention and AIDS transmission are three such issues.
3. We do need to be askable adults when our clients ask about more than what may be taught to them in the classroom. Personal fears, intimate concerns, emotional concerns about love, intimacy, sexual pleasure and even sexual techniques may not be included in every social-sexual curriculum but do need to be explained when clients or their parents ask about those matters.
4. It is good to affirm that sex between adequately mature and consenting adults who are informed and responsible can be pleasurable and rewarding for both people and even fun.
5. It is also important that you not be untrue to your own beliefs. If you believe that sexual activity must take place only between married adults, there is no reason for you to encourage sexual activity between unmarried adults. However, even if you have that belief, you will also have to realize that sex has and will take place in situations that you may not approve of, between individuals who do not meet your standards, and in other ways that may go beyond your comfort level or go against your moral, ethical or intellectual belief system. As a teacher or counselor, your job may be to deal with it. **If you are not comfortable teaching certain sexual topics or advocating your client's rights and point of view, it is your responsibility to find someone who can assist your student, client or son/daughter.** There can be guidance without prejudice or judgment.
Consider for example if a same-sex couple approached you for help regarding their sex life. If you had difficulties in accepting homosexuality, it would be appropriate for you to find a counselor who was comfortable dealing with these issues.
6. What makes a baby? Review this with the class or ask each person, "What makes a baby?" Ask each person individually.

a. Does kissing make a baby?
b. Does touching private parts with hands or fingers make a baby?
c. Does a man putting his finger inside a woman's vagina make a baby?
d. Does going into the wrong bathroom make a baby?
e. Does falling in love make a baby?
f. Does eating too much food make a baby?
g. Does oral sex make a baby?
h. Does masturbation make a baby?
i. Does sexual intercourse (a penis in a vagina) make a baby?
j. Does anal intercourse make a baby?

ANAL INTERCOURSE

Activity: Group Discussion
Say: "Raise your hand if you have ever had anal sex?" (Use an anatomy chart)
1. What is an anus?
2. Where is it?
3. Does everyone have one?
4. What is it normally used for?
5. Definition of anal intercourse: Anal intercourse is inserting a penis into a female's or male's anus. This is called anal intercourse or sodomy.
6. In private ask individuals who raised their hands earlier: "Is that what you did to someone" or "Is that what someone did to you? Did you want to do it?" If they say or indicate no, ask if they want to talk about it or want help. If your student or client was not a consenting adult or is confused about the issue it is necessary to seek professional assistance.
7. For some people, anal intercourse is pleasurable.
8. The risk of transmitting STD, particularly AIDS, is greater with unprotected anal intercourse than with vaginal intercourse.

HOW DO YOU KNOW WHEN YOU'RE READY FOR SEXUAL INTERCOURSE?

There is no set age or time when persons can be told that they are ready for sexual intercourse. It's an individual decision according to one's maturity and readiness. For some couples it is only appropriate if they are married. A case in point is the following story about Bob, one of my clients.

Bob, a dignified 67-year-old man and member of our Feeling Good socialization group at the sheltered workshop where he was employed shared with me on our way to lunch, "Gloria, I have been thinking about the things we have been learning about sexuality. Here I am, ending the years of my life and I have never known what it is like to make love with a woman."

I was touched by his sincerity. With great trepidation I shared with him information that I had learned in the medical community. There was a woman who specialized in having sex with disabled men. She did this for a fee. Bob perked up and asked, "How much does she charge?"

I said I would find out for him. I inquired and learned that she charged $75. I decided to wait until Bob brought up the subject again. At lunch, eight months later, he did. When I told him that she charged $75, he raised his eyebrows and thought about it for a moment. Then he replied, "Seventy-five dollars... Gloria, I think I'd rather use that money and go to Disneyland."

If your clients think they are ready for sexual intercourse then they must be ready for sexual responsibility. This includes birth control, STD prevention, awareness of appropriate sexual and social behavior, understanding the meaning of public and private and understanding the full meaning of having permission from their partner.

SHOULD YOU WAIT TO HAVE SEXUAL INTERCOURSE?

Yes. The first time someone has sex is an important decision. Being rushed or forced to have sex does no one any good. We encourage students to wait. There is a greater possibility of having a positive experience if an individual has had the opportunity to experience life and learn about themself before engaging in a sexual relationship. Knowing yourself emotionally and physically, knowing what you want and what you don't want, is a valuable prerequisite to a mature, responsible and satisfying sexual relationship.

PREGNANCY

Pregnant means that inside a woman, within her uterus (womb), a little egg is growing bigger and is becoming a baby. When a girl becomes a woman (review puberty) she produces an egg once a month. This egg moves from her ovary, through her Fallopian tube, into her uterus. When a man puts his penis into that woman's vagina at that time of the month, his sperm can fertilize her egg and that egg can then grow and become a baby. It takes nine months for an egg to become a full-sized baby. When the baby is ready, the baby is born. Being born means that the baby comes out of its mother's uterus through her vagina. If the mother or the baby has a problem at that time, the baby can be removed from it's mother's uterus with an operation done at a hospital.

We have not included detailed information on the physiology of pregnancy nor of menstruation or birth in this guidebook. This information is presented in many of the books listed in the Resources and in most libraries. Pregnancy may present specific problems for persons with certain disabilities.

Activity: Discussion Questions For Review
1. Who knows what "pregnant" means?
2. Can men become pregnant? Can women?
3. Can boys or girls become pregnant?
4. What is a virgin?
5. Can boys be virgins as well as girls?
6. How can someone get pregnant?
7. What is intercourse? What exactly is involved?
8. Do people have to have sex?
9. How do we know if we can trust others who want to have sexual intercourse with us? Who decides?
10. Is it OK to force someone or be forced to have sexual intercourse?
11. What if someone asks you to keep a secret about having sex or sexual intercourse with them?
12. What if they threaten you: "If you tell, then I'll…" What can you do? What are your choices?
13. How do you know when you're ready for sex, for intercourse? Make up a step-by-step checklist for readiness for the individual and for the couple in a relationship.
14. What are some considerations?
    a. who decides?
    b. who is responsible?

  c. what are the responsibilities involved?
15. Is it okay not to have intercourse?
16. What does pregnant mean?
17. How do you know if you are not pregnant?
18. How do you know if you are pregnant?
    a. do you have to hear a second heartbeat?
    b. do you have to be nauseated?
    c. does liking pickles with milk or ice cream mean you're pregnant?
19. What do you do if you think you might be pregnant?
20. What would you do if you were definitely pregnant?
21. What would you do if your girlfriend got pregnant?
22. To whom could you talk?
23. To whom couldn't you talk?
24. Do nice people have unwanted pregnancies?
25. How long can you safely wait before finding out if you're pregnant?
26. If you think you are ready for sexual intercourse, you must be ready for sexual responsibility. What are those responsibilities?

PARENTHOOD

Before discussing any of the details of pregnancy, the first question to ask is if the individuals are ready to become parents.

Consider the situation of a 19-year-old woman with a developmental disability whose dream was to be "normal." To her, being "normal" meant getting married and having children.

By itself, this dream might seem inappropriate and even a little bit frightening to her family or to her social worker. Do they want a woman with mental retardation to bring children into the world when this woman is not even able to take care of her own needs?

An initial response might be to tell her that her dream is unrealistic and then do whatever possible to discourage her. But in reality what her family would want for her and what her social worker would want for her would be for her to become more independent, more capable, more "normal" and thereby better able to do what would be required of a parent.

No dream is unrealistic if the realization of the dream will benefit everyone. Both society and this woman will benefit by working towards this dream. Oscar Hammerstein said it to Richard Rodgers' music: "If you don't have a dream, how you gonna have a dream come true?"

People who have dreams and who believe in their dreams are people who are productive individuals. When fulfillment of their dreams benefits others as well as themselves, these people evolve and blossom with excitement that draws others towards them and towards the fulfillment of their dreams. The dream provides a context or a matrix for the direction of their life. Reality is often dependent on what the majority of people say and agree is real. This means that when you are willing and lucky to find enough people with whom you can share your dream, you can make your own dream real.

"Nothing in life just happens. It isn't enough to believe in something; you have to have the stamina to meet obstacles and overcome them, to struggle." (Golda Meir)

As you continue to live and develop your dream, the dream or the goal may evolve and change. That is to be expected. What is important is that the process of realization of the dream is itself life giving and affirming. The dream can inspire the energy and reinforce the self-confidence needed to learn the skills that will be needed for its fulfillment. Are the dreamer and the dream really separate?

In fact, with what this 19-year-old woman will need to learn in order to become a capable parent, she might even gain enough insight to decide not to have children herself. Rather than deny her dream, it is so much more valuable to go with her dream and use it to assist her to progress into adulthood.

Working towards her dream would include that she first learn such skills as:
1. How to take care of her own personal hygiene.
2. How to dress herself and take care of her own clothing so that she would later do this for her child.
3. How to make her own bed and clean and organize her own apartment.
4. How to earn money and use money and make change,
5. How to get out of the house and meet other people and learn social skills.
6. How to shop for food, for clothes, how to use public transportation (all skills that she will need if she chooses to become a parent).
7. How to use the telephone and express herself clearly.
8. How to protect herself from physical exploitation.

As she begins to acquire those skills, she might be given the opportunity to take care of some little children perhaps as a mother's helper. She would have the opportunity to diaper babies and take care of them when they cry. As a result of this training (training which, by the way, is valuable for everyone who would want to become a parent), she might want to delay having her own children or not have them at all. On the other hand, if she were able to learn these skills (and in fact she might very well be able to acquire all those skills although it might take her longer than someone else), she might be able to become a capable spouse and parent.

It is good to remember that "All the way to heaven is heaven." (Anonymous)
The process can be the goal.

"Ah but a man's reach should exceed his grasp, or what's a heaven for?"
(Robert Browning).

Activity: Group Discussion – Responsibilities in Child Care
The following exercise is intentionally slanted towards the difficulties and complexities involved in parenting to discourage the idea of becoming pregnant and having to raise children which is a difficult although not impossible task for a couple or individual with (or without) mental retardation.
1. Ask group what the mother and the father have to do to take care of a baby:
    a. Why does a baby cry?
        (1. The baby may have dirty diapers. Ask if anyone has ever changed diapers. Point out what a mess they are and that they must be washed and dried (much work). If they suggest disposable diapers, point out that they're expensive.
        (2. The baby may be hungry. Point out how parents have to know what is good food and how to prepare that food correctly for their baby. Warm milk, for example, cannot be too hot or it will burn the baby's mouth.
        (3. The baby may be sick. The baby could be hurting anywhere but not be able to tell you. How would you know what to do?
    b. How would anyone in class know why baby was crying for (1, (2. or (3?

c. How much would it cost to clean or buy diapers, buy food, go to a doctor? Point out it all costs a lot of money.
   d. A baby needs someone there <u>all the time</u>. It is difficult for parents to go to movies or parties or sleep through the night and there is little money left after baby's expenses.
2. If some students claim to be able to handle the cost, ask them, "Where will the money come from?"
3. Ask, "Who can take care of a baby when it's sick or injured? Who knows what to do if a baby:
   a. Coughs blood?"
   b. Swallows poison?"
   c. Falls down stairs?"
   d. Stops breathing?" (etc.)
4. Ask, "Who has enough money to:
   a. Buy all the food for their family?"
   b. Buy all their own clothes?"
   c. Pay rent for family?"
   d. Pay doctor bills?"
   e. Pay for medicines?"
5. Ask students, "What would happen to your baby if you didn't have enough money for:
   a. Food (starve)."
   b. Clothes (look bad; maybe get cold, sick)."
   c. A doctor (could die)."
   d. Rent (have no place to live; get rained on, snowed on, get cold, get sick, still no money for doctor, etc.)."
6. Ask students, "What would happen to your baby if it:
   a. Had no food?"
   b. Had no clothes?"
7. Ask, "Who wants to have a baby and let it:
   a. Starve to death?"
   b. Get sick and die?"
8. Ask the class: "Is anyone here ready to have a baby?" If there are "yes" answers, ask the group if they think that student is ready to have a baby. Allow for as much peer pressure as possible. Point out that their own parents are not likely to want to raise more children.
9. Wrap up activity, pointing out that parents must:
   a. Have money to pay for things (list again).
   b. Know what to do in an emergency and be able to do it. Give examples.
10. You may not want to become parents but you might feel ready to have sexual intercourse, in which case you must be ready for sexual responsibility to prevent pregnancy and STD.

BIRTH CONTROL

***Maturity level*: age 13+**
1. Individual vs. Mutual Responsibility
A person with a disability may have difficulty applying or inserting any mechanical or chemical contraceptive. If hormonal methods are contraindicated, the non or less disabled partner may be able to apply or insert the contraceptive for his or her partner. Alternately, the non or less disabled partner may have to use the

appropriate contraceptive. Whoever does what, it is both partners who share the responsibility for birth control and the prevention of STD transmission.
2. Review the discussion regarding responsibilities for child care (pg. 105).
3. Effectiveness of Birth Control Methods
For medical or other reasons, the absolute prevention of conception may be more important to persons with a disability than to individuals without a disability.

METHODS OF BIRTH CONTROL
1. Chemical.
    a. Spermicidal creams, jellies and foams used by themselves are fairly effective. They do not offer reliable protection against STD.
2. Mechanical.
    a. A rubber condom is highly effective when used properly and never reused. It offers effective STD protection as well.
    b. Diaphragm with spermicide is highly effective. The diaphragm works by virtue of containing the spermicidal agent against the mouth of the cervix. Although mechanical, it is not by itself a barrier to sperm. It does not offer reliable protection against STD.
3. IUD (intrauterine device).
    Inserted into the woman by a physician as a minor in-office surgical procedure, it is highly (but not absolutely) effective for birth control. It provides no protection against STD.
4. Hormonal.
    a. Birth control pills with different combinations of estrogens and progesterones are effective. Ovulation is completely prevented. Some may be used to stop all menstruation if that is desired for easier vaginal hygiene.
    b. Injection of slow release progesterone (depot-medroxyprogesterone acetate) provides three months' protection. There are occasional side effects in some persons with spasticity such as increase in spasm.
    c. Contraceptive Skin Patch is a small (1.75 square inch) adhesive patch worn on the skin. It must be changed weekly.
    d. The "Morning After Pill" contains a high dose of the hormones used in ordinary birth control pills. It is effective if taken within 72 hours after intercourse. It must be prescribed by a physician but legislation allowing pharmacists to dispense this without a prescription in being considered.
    e. Hormonal contraception provides no protection against STD.
5. Rhythm method.
    Merely counting the days after menstruation to find the so-called "safe time" is rarely effective and often leads to unplanned pregnancy (people who use the rhythm method for contraception are usually called "parents"). There are some women who can clearly sense their own ovulation ("mittelschmertz"). There are methods of determining ovulation using special thermometers and charts. There are tests of cervical mucus to ascertain fertile times. We do not recommend the rhythm method but if this is the only method acceptable, consult a gynecologist to learn the necessary details. This provides no protection against STD.
6. Withdrawal method.
    The couple has unprotected intercourse and the male withdraws just before he ejaculates. This is totally unreliable. The pre-ejaculatory fluid secreted by the male can carry live sperm. In moments of passion, withdrawal in time, all the time, is rarely guaranteed. It also provides no protection against STD.
7. Sterilization.
    Totally effective and usually permanent but offers no protection against STD.

a. A simple surgical procedure for men called vasectomy, the tube (the vas deferens) that brings sperm from the testicles to the prostate gland is divided and tied through a small incision made in the scrotum. The man can still experience orgasm and ejaculation but there will be no sperm in the fluid he releases. The procedure is performed easily in a doctor's office and is permanently effective. Reversing the procedure is extremely difficult (and more expensive) and often unsuccessful.
b. Women can be sterilized by tubal ligation, tying off and dividing the Fallopian tubes. This procedure can be done with a laparoscope (a minimally invasive operation done through a small puncture next to the belly button). It is also permanent. Reversing the procedure to allow pregnancy is more difficult (and more expensive) and is not always successful.
c. Hysterectomy (removal of the uterus) also makes pregnancy impossible permanently. It cannot be reversed. It is a major surgical procedure.
d. Sterilization provides no protection against transmission of STD.

HOW TO DECIDE ON THE BEST METHOD OF BIRTH CONTROL?
An experienced and humane gynecologist can give the best advice in individual situations. Planned Parenthood is a reliable resource for advice and educational guidance.

HOW TO TEACH THE USE OF BIRTH CONTROL METHODS
TO INDIVIDUALS WHO ARE SLOW LEARNERS

1. Condoms:
    a. Male students practice opening the condom packet and rolling the condom onto the penis. Commonly, plastic or rubber models of the erect penis are used for demonstration. However, it may not follow that all slow learners can generalize the information to apply it to life situations. Teaching individual students to do this on themselves can be difficult because a penis needs to be erect in order for a condom to be applied. It may be helpful to show a video that demonstrates the technique.
    b. Female students also need to understand how men use condoms properly as the device protects the woman. A female is responsible to protect herself by making sure that the man is using a new condom and using it properly. Female students can practice opening the packet and practice applying it to a plastic model of an erect penis as well as watching the video. The teacher or group leader will need to decide if the video should be shown to coed classes or if the classes should be segregated.
2. Diaphragms:
    Plastic or rubber models can be used as well as videos. Since these are prescription devices, each woman will need to be fitted by a physician or nurse practitioner that can demonstrate how it's done. The patient must then practice inserting the diaphragm herself and the nurse or doctor must be sure that she can do it properly including use of the spermicidal cream or jelly.
3. Birth control pills:
    May be discussed with students in a classroom. Since these are prescription medications, each woman will need to see a physician or nurse practitioner. Women who are slow learners may be forgetful and will need a system that works to insure that they take the pills properly. Taking all the pills at once or just taking them when they have sexual intercourse is not the proper way.

4. IUDs and hormone injections:
   These can also be discussed in the classroom and also will be prescribed, inserted or administered by a physician or nurse.

To learn more about birth control, we suggest that you invite a Planned Parenthood educator or your local Family Planning Organization who are trained to work with people who are slow learners to meet with you, your staff and your groups.

STD (SEXUALLY TRANSMITTED DISEASE) INCLUDING AIDS

The following are specific objectives for learning:
1. To learn about the most common sexually transmitted diseases (STDs).
2. To learn what parts of the body are affected by STDs.
3. To learn how to prevent the spread of STD.
4. To learn what to do if exposed to STD.
5. To learn ways to teach about STD to slow learners.
6. To learn what Acquired Immune Deficiency (AIDS) is.
7. To learn how AIDS is transmitted.

Maturity level: age 12+

When the first edition of this book was published in 1977, sexually transmitted diseases were called "venereal diseases." There were a limited number of these diseases. All of them had effective treatments. Most were completely curable.

Those diseases are still with us and treatment for most of them is even more effective. Of greater significance is that new, more deadly sexually transmitted diseases have since appeared. It is well beyond the scope of this book to provide detailed explanations about all the STDs and how they are treated. Within this curriculum we want to teach our students and clients the importance and the techniques of preventing the spread of disease. The following is a basic primer meant to answer some of the questions that a sex educator might want to know about certain STDs. To learn more, we recommend that you refer to the Resource information at the end of this book.

STDs are diseases that are passed from one individual to another by sexual activity. This means that the infecting agent is passed during acts of sexual intercourse (vaginal or anal), fellatio or cunnilingus (oral sex).

With many STDs there are sores on or near the genitalia of one partner that shed living germs (bacteria, fungus or virus) that infect broken or damaged skin on or near the genitalia (or mouth) of the other partner. In some cases the infection may be passed from one to another in semen, vaginal fluid or blood, including menstrual fluid. These include certain types of the hepatitis virus as well as the HIV (human immunodeficiency) virus, the cause of AIDS (Acquired Immune Deficiency Syndrome). Some of these diseases are transmitted more readily than others. Some of these diseases can be cured. Those that cannot be cured can be treated. All of these diseases can be prevented.

DEFINITION
STD refers to infections that are passed from one person to another by direct sexual contact (may be heterosexual or homosexual).

AREAS OF THE BODY THAT DIFFERENT STDs CAN AFFECT
1. Females
    a. genitalia, including vulva, Bartholin's glands, urethra, vagina and skin surrounding the genitalia.
    b. internal organs, including uterus (uncommon), fallopian tubes, ovaries.
    c. other areas of sexual contact, including anus and rectum, mouth, pharynx (including tonsils).
    d. secondary areas of infection: bloodstream, lymph nodes, joints (arthritis), liver (hepatitis), and other organs (AIDS).
2. Males
    a. genitalia, including penis, urethra, scrotum and surrounding skin.
    b. internal organs, including prostate gland, seminal vesicles, epididymis, testicles.
    c. other areas of sexual contact, including anus and rectum, mouth, pharynx including tonsils.
    d. secondary areas of infection: bloodstream, lymph nodes, joints (arthritis), liver (hepatitis), and other organs (AIDS).

PREVENTION OF STD
1. Honest Communication. If both sexual partners are open with each other and have been recently tested, they will each know if the other has had any risk of exposure from anyone else.
2. Abstinence from sexual contact. Intentions to refrain from sexual contact are often overcome, forgotten or neglected in the heat of arousal or a consequence of emotional immaturity and thus preparation for the prevention of disease transmission are vitally important, perhaps life saving.
3. Sexual contact other than sexual or anal intercourse (for example: mutual masturbation) lowers the risk of transmission of most STDs
4. Rubber condoms used properly reduce risk for most STDs.

WHAT TO DO IF EXPOSED TO STD
See a doctor or a clinic. (One hopes that your doctor will not only be medically competent but understanding as well.) Tell your partner!

Activity: Teaching People Who Are Slow Learners About STD
Materials: Models (or photos or drawings) of genitalia
    Rubber STD sores (or photos, drawings of genitalia with sores)
    Rubber cement
    Photographs of authority figures (doctors, nurses, priests, teachers, parents, policemen, firemen)
1. Ask students if any of them have ever been sick or hurt.
    a. "What did it feel like?"
    b. "Where did it hurt?"
    c. "When do you go to the doctor?"
2. Display models (or photos or drawings) of penis and vagina with sores.
    a. "This man has a sore on his penis. Should he go to the doctor?"
    b. "This woman has a sore on her vagina. Should she go to the doctor?"
    c. "If you get sores on your penis or your vagina, you should go to the doctor."
3. Remove sores from models (or show images) of penis and vagina without sores and say:

a. "This man's penis looks OK, but when he urinates (pees) his penis hurts. It feels like it stings or burns. Should he go to the doctor?" Ask all male students: "Should you go to the doctor if your penis hurts when you urinate?"
   b. "This woman's vagina looks OK, but it hurts (or feels like burning) when she urinates (pees). This woman has noticed an unpleasant smell coming from her vagina. Should she go to the doctor?"
4. Hold up photographs of authority figures including doctors (male and female), nurses, priests, teachers, parents, policemen, firemen. Instruct male students to place model (or photo or drawing) of penis; and instruct female students to place model of vagina; with the photograph of the person they would tell if they felt or noticed sores on their genital area or experienced burning sensations when they urinated.
5. Explain that people who have intercourse <u>might</u> develop STD.
   a. Allow students to relate stories.
   b. Always ask if the illness or injury was serious enough for them to go to the doctor.
6. Exhibit model of healthy vagina and penis with sores (STD).
   a. State that the woman will get STD if she puts the penis in her vagina.
   b. Then show vagina with STD sores.
7. Repeat process with model of healthy penis and vagina with sores (STD).
8. State that using a condom (show condom on model of penis) helps stop STD. Review how to find, buy and use a condom.
10. Say, "If you get STD you are sick. You must go to the doctor. If you don't go to the doctor, you could get very sick or even die."
11. Repeat that the use of a condom helps prevent STD.

   This is a difficult topic to teach to people who are severely retarded. At one extreme it could lead to blind fear of any sexual activity. This might seem like a desirable outcome when the consequences of careless sexual activity can be severe. At another extreme it might be so complicated that the student just ignores the entire message.
   If the student or client is less severely retarded, it may be possible to teach more options, more variables. For instance, sexual activity between consenting adults who know each other and are monogamous and have not had prior exposure to STD or who have been tested, can be safe. For example: a married couple who are honest and faithful to one another. For those students you might teach also about abnormal urethral discharges rather than just speaking about sores and burning. Also you may point out that people do not always see sores or notice symptoms. Regular check-ups with their doctors can also help prevent problems.

SPECIFIC STDs

1. **Syphilis** (lues, bad blood) is caused by a spirochete, an organism larger than a bacterium but smaller than a parasite. It occurs in four forms:
   a. Primary syphilis: a chancre, a small non-tender lesion with an ulcerated center appears for a short time at the area of contact (usually on skin of genitalia, near rectum, lips) 3 to 5 days after contact.
   b. Secondary syphilis: skin rash over most of the body; appears after 2 to 4 weeks and is highly infectious at this time.
   c. Tertiary syphilis: brain, spine and/or heart damage.
   d. Congenital syphilis: passed in utero from mother to fetus causes congenital defects and damage similar to tertiary.

      e. Syphilis is usually diagnosed with blood tests. It can be cured when treated early with antibiotics. Tertiary syphilis may be incurable and congenital syphilis may be untreatable.
2. **Gonorrhea** (clap, drip, haircut) is caused by bacteria.
    a. In males it causes painful or burning urination and usually but not always a discharge of pus from the urethra. It can lead to urethral strictures.
    b. In females there are frequently no symptoms. Untreated it can cause sterility.
    c. In males and females it can also cause tonsillitis and arthritis.
    d. Rectal infection may cause few or no symptoms.
    e. Gonorrhea is diagnosed by microscopic examination and culture of the urethral discharge. It can be cured with antibiotics.
3. **Other STDs** include **chlamydia, genital herpes (herpes simplex virus - hsv), genital warts (human papilloma virus - hpv)** and **trichomoniasis**.
    a. Diagnosis of these conditions is by physical examination and laboratory tests.
    b. Sexually active women should be checked annually for chlamydia by their physician. It is now considered one of the most common causes of infertility.
    c. Effective treatments are available for these conditions.
    d. If any of your clients experience symptoms such as: **burning with urination, vaginal burning, discharge, itch, bad or peculiar odor, sores or other lesions around the genitalia or rectum, or swollen glands in the groin,** it is advisable to take those clients to a qualified physician or clinic for prompt diagnosis and treatment. Since several of these infections can occur without sexual contact (for instance some are associated with extended antibiotic usage) there need not be embarrassment nor shame. While some of these infections are only physically unpleasant, some are "silent" but can lead to sterility or other more serious consequences. If the infection was sexually transmitted, it is important to notify and treat the partner(s) as well. These "problems" may then become opportunities for education.
4. **Hepatitis**
    Infection of the liver, called hepatitis, is caused by at least five viruses and possibly six (A, B, C, D, E and possibly G). Each has a different pattern of transmission. Some are STDs, some are not.
    a. **Hepatitis A.** Unprotected sexual contact is <u>not</u> ordinarily associated with transmission of hepatitis A. It is most commonly transmitted when an individual ingests food or water that is fecally contaminated. Some cases are related to the ingestion of raw shellfish. Increased risk for infection is seen with certain institutional workers including caretakers for developmentally challenged people and employees of child day-care centers. Vaccination offers long-term immunity to hepatitis A and is recommended for groups at risk.
    b. **Hepatitis B** is most commonly transmitted by transfusion of contaminated blood or blood products or by using contaminated needles (for instance with intravenous drug abuse). Unprotected contact (including vaginal and anal intercourse and receptive oral sex) are the most risky sexual behaviors that transmit the virus. All non-monogamous sexually active individuals as well as all heath care workers who come into contact with blood or blood products should be vaccinated.
    c. **Hepatitis C** transmission by sexual activity is uncommon but condoms should be used in short-term sexual relationships. No vaccine is yet available.

d. The **other types of hepatitis (D, E and G)** are uncommon in the United States. Transmission is by varied routes including intrafamilial contact, sexual contact and ingestion of contaminated food or water.

5. **AIDS**

   In July 1981, a small article in The New York Times reported the outbreak of a rare "cancer" among 41 gay men in New York and California. Few people imagined that an epidemic of monumental proportion was imminent.[*]

   Since then more than 22 million men, women and children worldwide have died of AIDS, and an estimated 40 million people are living with HIV. AIDS affects people of all ethnicities, genders and sexual orientations. While the risk of contacting AIDS may be greater among persons who engage in risky behavior, the risk is there for everyone because the virus can be passed not only by illicit or extra-marital sex, but by any sexual activity if one of the partners has the disease, known or unknown. It can be passed from a pregnant mother to her fetus. It can be passed by blood transfusion (but NOT by donating blood), or by using dirty or contaminated needles for any purpose.

   AIDS means Acquired Immune Deficiency Syndrome.
   It is caused by HIV, Human Immunodeficiency Virus.
   It can be treated.

THE BIOLOGY OF SEXUAL TRANSMISSION OF HIV

HIV may be transmitted sexually when HIV in one partner's semen, cervical/vaginal fluid or blood comes into contact with the bloodstream or mucous membranes of another partner. HIV antibodies can usually be detected by blood tests within 12 weeks after exposure and in almost all cases by six months.

FACTORS AFFECTING SEXUAL TRANSMISSION
While three-quarters or more of all HIV infections are transmitted sexually, transmission does not occur during every unprotected sexual contact. Sexual transmission is a product of the interaction of a wide range of host, viral and environmental factors.

Transmissibility is influenced both by the infectiousness of the source partner and the susceptibility of the recipient partner. Newly infected persons are more likely to transmit HIV than those at later stages of the disease, especially during the period before their blood tests turn positive. Other factors that may influence infectiousness include pregnancy and phase of the menstrual cycle.

Transmission is more likely when there is damage or injury to the mucous membranes. In men, greater susceptibility has been associated with non-circumcision. In women, greater susceptibility has been associated with higher vaginal pH (a more acidic vaginal environment is protective against infection). Cervical ectopy (the presence of a certain type of cell on the cervix, particularly common in young women) and IUD use may make women more susceptible to infection. The presence of STDs can also increase both infectiousness and susceptibility to HIV.

---

[*] Taken from the Bulletin of Experimental Treatments for AIDS, Summer 1999 issue, by Liz Highleyman, published by the San Francisco AIDS Foundation.

ANAL, VAGINAL, ORAL SEX; HOW RISKY ARE THEY?

Different sexual acts are associated with varying likelihoods of transmitting HIV. Anal intercourse has the highest potential for transmitting the virus because the rectal lining is thinner and more prone to minor damage. Next most risky is unprotected vaginal intercourse. The receptive partner is at a significantly higher risk than the insertive partner because the receptive partner accepts semen into the rectum or vagina, allowing prolonged contact with mucous membranes.

Oral sex carries a much lower risk of HIV transmission than anal or vaginal intercourse. The risk is increased if the receptive partner has gum disease (such as bleeding gums), other oral infections or injuries in his or her mouth and if the receptive partner is menstruating. Female-to-female transmission of HIV is theoretically possible but rare.

What is the message here? Today, sexual behavior is far more risky than it ever was. And yet there is still the natural urge and natural attraction to sexual activity that has been with our species and our predecessor species since the first animals appeared on the earth. As parents and teachers raising children, we teach them right and wrong, we teach them survival skills, we teach them about love. As parents and teachers of individuals with developmental delays, that teaching process is more challenging. Just as we teach youngsters not to play in traffic and we remind them to fasten their seatbelts because of the risks, we must teach our children, students and clients with developmental delays what risks they face as they grow into maturity. Sexual activity with another person requires preparation and readiness. Part of that is the understanding of the consequences of making the wrong choices or making mistakes. Use the information provided here for your own reference as you teach your students or clients about STD.

Activity: Summary Discussion of STD

Discussion questions:
1. How do you get STD?
2. What is "direct sexual contact"?
3. Do toilet seats spread STD?
4. Do clean people pass on STD?
5. Do nice people pass on STD?
6. Do people you know pass on STD?
7. How do you know if you have STD?
8. What should you do if you think you have STD?
9. How can you prevent STD?

HOMOSEXUALITY

Maturity level: age 12+

The following are specific objectives for learning:
1. To know what homosexuality is
2. To become familiar with the myths associated with homosexuality
3. To understand the difference between *situational* and *constitutional* homosexuality
4. To be able to distinguish the difference between homo*sexual* and homo*sensual* feelings or activity
5. To become aware of sexual barriers in same-sex behavior
6. To express feelings about same-sex behavior
7. To become familiar with bisexual behavior

8. To become acquainted with terminology used to identify and understand different homosexually related behavior
9. To explain and discuss the difference between homosexual exploration when growing up and homosexual activity as an adult by choice
10. To discuss homosexuality as a pre-determined sexual orientation, just as heterosexuality is a pre-determined sexual orientation

Homosexuality more than any other topic may inspire strong judgmental attitudes, moralizations and anxieties, probably more so with administrators and parents than with the children or clients. More than any other style of sexual interaction, same-sex behavior may be the most convenient for patients confined to hospital wards or clients in facilities segregated by sex. It is the only style of behavior where reproduction, which may be strongly medically contraindicated, is absolutely impossible, perhaps making same-sex practice more convenient and desirable than opposite-sex interactions. This is not to endorse any sexual preference or to condemn it but to explore, evaluate and understand it.

The words that are politically correct may change from time to time. Homosexual men are (now) properly described as gay. Homosexual women are called lesbians.

HOMOSEXUALITY AS A SEXUAL ORIENTATION

It is useful to view homosexuality as being **constitutional** or **situational**. **Constitutional homosexuality** implies that the person is sexually attracted to people of the same sex not by conscious choice but because the individual feels that attraction naturally and spontaneously and doesn't feel that same attraction for members of the opposite sex. Most authorities now believe that this orientation is determined by the age of five or younger and does not change thereafter. It is not known what causes this orientation. It may be genetically pre-determined.

Situational homosexuality describes sexual attraction to the same sex as a result of the unavailability of the opposite sex. This is a situation common in prisons, in boarding schools, in residential hospitals and other same-sex residential facilities. When members of the opposite sex are accessible, heterosexual attraction replaces the homosexual attraction.

Situational heterosexuality could be a phenomenon if a constitutional homosexual had no member of the same sex available as a partner. Sometimes, a constitutional homosexual person marries a person of the opposite sex to satisfy certain societal roles or out of fear of his or her own homosexuality.

"Coming out" is a phrase used to describe the process of discontinuing the hiding of one's homosexual orientation. It is a process that many homosexual men and women approach with great anxiety. What would be the reactions from their parents, their friends, their work associates, their bosses? And yet in the experience of many such people it is usually a necessary process in freeing oneself from living a lie.

Many young people are terribly confused by their own attraction to people of the same sex and upset by the lack of their own interest (especially erotic interest) in the "normal" object of sexual desire, a person of the opposite sex. They may feel terribly alone and isolated because their only knowledge of such people is that they are "queers" or "faggots" and they deserve only to be hated or beaten up. People all around them are almost universally contemptuous of "homos," and since no one will admit to same-sex preference, they have no apparent choice but to feel secretive, guilty and ashamed.

It is important to understand that many males and females have homosexual experiences during their adolescence. A few experiences do not make the person homosexual. A homosexual person is best defined as one who, as an adult, realizes that his or her sexual preferences are for members of the same sex. There are over 28 million homosexual men and women in the United States, nearly one in ten Americans.

Activity: Discussion - What is a Homosexual?

The teacher gives examples of situations associated with common myths and asks the students to decide if the person or people involved would be considered lesbians or homosexuals and how they feel about each example. Some examples may include:

1. Lucy and Ethel on "I Love Lucy" or other same-sex friends on popular TV series.
2. Two teenagers who enjoy swimming nude together.
3. A young man wearing an earring.
4. Two men walking down the street holding hands (You may point out later that this is common behavior in various parts of the world today, including the Middle East).
5. Two men greeting each other by kissing on the lips.
6. Two women kissing each other on the lips as they meet.
7. A man who massages men at a sports club.
8. A man who *gets* massaged by a man at a sports club.

Explain the difference between homo*sensual* behavior and homo*sexual* behavior. An individual may enjoy the affection and the touch of another individual of the same sex without having any interest in or attraction to having sexual relations with that individual. Football team members may hug one another enthusiastically, wrestlers may compete against one another, women friends may help each other to try on clothing and all may enjoy those activities without being homosexual.

Ask the class to indicate examples of same-sex behavior that bothers them; that turns them on. List these examples on the chalkboard. In society, same-sex behavior among men is usually more disturbing than same-sex behavior with women. Discuss male image and roles in society.

Activity: Explore your own sexual barriers with the same sex.
Maturity level: age 17+

1. Hand out papers with drawings of two girls, titled: "Good Friend." Label one drawing "in public." Label the other drawing: "in private." Do the same with the male figures. (No need to write pupil's name on sheet. Indicate only the sex of the student with an M or F.)
2. Ask students to shade in the parts of the body he or she would feel comfortable touching depending on the sex of the friend and whether the touching occurred in public or private. (Allow each student privacy during this exercise.)
3. When the class finishes, put the papers shaded by boys in one pile and those shaded by girls in a separate pile.
4. Invite the students to inspect piles separately and invite their responses.
5. Some leading questions may include:
    a. Are there differences in the body parts the boys and girls shaded in?
    b. Are there differences in the boys' responses? The girls' responses?
    c. Do boys seem more or less comfortable touching someone of their own sex?
6. Experiments for social awareness of homosexual behavior:
    a. Have boys pair off and girls pair off.
        *(1. Boys hold hands or put their arms around each others' waists and walk together down the halls.

        (2. Girls do the same.
  b. Share feelings and reactions.
  c. Ask girls how they felt seeing the boys holding hands and vice-versa.
  d. Discuss news articles concerning two men or two women who applied for a marriage license, or other current events concerning homosexuality.

BISEXUAL BEHAVIOR
Activity: Discussion
1. Can a person like boys and girls? (Men and women?)
2. Can they love both men and women?
3. Can they enjoy sensual and/or sexual activity with both men and women?
4. How do you feel about it?
   Discuss how we are all bisexual in certain ways. Reexamine the exercises and drawings used previously. It is usually just a matter of degrees of preference for different behavior.

     Dr. Alfred Kinsey described sexual preference as scanning a full spectrum from zero percent homosexual to 100 percent homosexual with the great majority of us fitting somewhere in between. Most of us have some attraction for members of both sexes but with a preference (which may be stronger or weaker) for the opposite sex. This may be similar to other sets of preferences many of us have for sexual partners, preferences oriented toward body type, height, hip size or shape, chest size or shape, hair color, race, intellectual capacity or religious preference.
     The ultimate conclusions here about homosexuality will be to blur rather than to clarify the differences between homosexuality and heterosexuality. The goal is to become aware of the similarities in all of us, not the differences. The purpose of this is to decrease anxieties about labels by understanding that mixed and changing feelings in all of us are natural, common and okay. Problems most often arise when we do not accept what we feel within ourselves. If we accept these feelings then we can at least speak of them, share questions and ultimately allay our anxieties.

OTHER BEHAVIORS, LIFESTYLES AND CONDITIONS ASSOCIATED WITH HOMOSEXUALITY
1. **Transvestitism**: (cross-dressing): obtaining sexual gratification from dressing in clothes of the opposite sex. *Not* necessarily a homosexual behavior.
2. **Transsexualism**: the condition of people who have the conviction that they belong to the opposite sex. A transsexual is a person who lives the role of the opposite sex before or after surgical and legal sex reassignment. Most transsexuals are attracted to individuals of their same genetic sex but some are attracted to the opposite sex.
3. **Hermaphroditism**: the coexistence in an individual of the sexual organs or vestiges of the sexual organs of both sexes. This is very rare in humans. It is more common in some animals and plants. Some organisms can actually change their sex in response to biological needs. It has no relationship to homosexuality.
4. **Female Impersonator**: male actor who takes the role of a female. May or may not be homosexual.
5. **In Drag**: a man dressing in the clothing of a female (usually dressed theatrically or otherwise outrageously).

SEXUAL INDEPENDENCE

The following are specific objectives for learning:

1. To share feelings and experiences about privacy and intimacy.
2. To become aware of individual physical limitations in areas of expression of and carrying out of intimate activities.
3. To become aware of psychological attitudes that limit intimate expressions.
4. To become aware of choices available that can help to allow expression in areas of affection and sexual contact.
5. To understand how persons with disabilities may be limited by those around them (parents, hospital personnel) from sexual expression or fulfilling sexual needs.
6. To know how to communicate sexual concerns to those who care for individuals with disabilities.
7. To understand the sexual rights of a person with disabilities.
8. To consider how a facilitator may assist a person or couple with disabilities to achieve sexual satisfaction.

The following is a situation in which a young adult who is severely physically disabled may find her or himself.

Here she (or he) is learning about her own sexuality, learning how to experiment and explore her own body and finding ways to experience sexual pleasure and satisfaction. For this to be satisfactorily experienced either alone or with a partner, she may wish this to be an intimate private experience. She may thus require a certain degree of independence from her family or from the institutional environment where she lives. She is also discovering physical limitations that make certain sexual choices or activities difficult.

Conflict may arise when this separateness is needed for feelings of intimacy or privacy but there still remains her physical dependence for bodily manipulations, positioning, dressing, etc. The problem may be further compounded if this experience is to be with a partner who is also severely physically handicapped. If the family or institutional attendants have not come to terms with sexuality for the handicapped family member or patient, you can imagine the discomfort everyone may experience.

This is a time (better before the occasion arises) when the individual with disabilities must get in touch with her rights as a sexual human being. This is also the time (better before the occasion arises) when the individual must be educated about the readiness and responsibilities of sexual activity with another person.

Two institutional residents with cerebral palsy expressed to the staff that they wanted to have sexual intercourse. They said that they were in love. Because they were each so severely physically handicapped, they were going to require significant assistance from the staff if they were to be able to carry this out. After much consideration, and because the staff felt such empathy for the couple, they facilitated sexual intercourse. Unfortunately, the couple had not really explored this advanced stage of sexual intimacy and they were not adequately prepared. They suffered months of shame and confusion and required therapy. The staff meant well but realized later that a tremendous amount of communication, sex education and processing of feelings and all the steps in between love and sexual intercourse were necessary for their sexual readiness.

There are no simple solutions to this kind of problem. All the activities outlined in preceding discussions are designed to enlighten individuals with disabilities, their parents and families, their teachers, their therapists and their hospital attendants about sexuality and its "normality." We have discussed different ways of expressing sexuality and most importantly we encourage all concerned parties to communicate freely about problems and expectations as well as anxieties. The goal is to enable all of us to deal with *people,* with *feelings,* with fantasies and desires, and with embarrassment.

Privacy and intimacy are very personal concepts and needs, meaning different things to different people. Make no assumptions. It is an area to explore and discuss openly with all concerned persons in order to gain understanding and clarity.

The objectives at the beginning of this section may be used as discussion topics. The answers to the questions are whatever answers develop from the discussion.

SEXUAL FACILITATOR

A brief word about the sexuality facilitator concept. A facilitator may be anyone that turns the lights low or hangs out the sign "Do Not Disturb" on a patient's door. It may be a person who rolls one patient's wheelchair into another patient's room and then discreetly leaves. With more trust and closeness it may be the attendant that undresses two patients who may be unable to undress themselves and lets them have some private time together in one patient's room. It could be a friend who helps a friend with severe physical disabilities to masturbate. Or it may be a friend who helps a disabled couple with disabilities who feel ready to experiment to position them for some kind of mutual sexual pleasuring.

Some people or institutions may be uncomfortable in allowing that kind of intimacy. Some may feel comfortable. Open communication between the person with disabilities and his or her attendant or facilitator will allow for many options. Mindfulness, caring, respect and sex education are absolute prerequisites. This must include education about relationships, how to know if you're really in love (sex is not love), the possible consequences of having sex when one or both individuals are not ready, and what to do if they discover they really weren't ready for sex but were ready for a deep and lasting friendship. This is true for everybody.

SENIOR CITIZENS

The language in this guide implies that the persons with whom it deals are young or are students. Certainly anyone who is searching for knowledge or awareness is a student and those of us that concern ourselves with bodies, with sensations, with sensuality or with sexuality is maintaining youthful interests. In that sense this guide is directed to the young at heart and to students. In truth, this book is designed for everybody including senior citizens. Seniors do not cease to feel or be sexual or cease to feel or be sensual. It is part of being alive.

However, like anyone who is disabled, the senior citizen who either <u>considers</u> himself or herself to be disabled by age or <u>is considered by others</u> to be disabled by age may be handicapped. Certain senior citizens may be institutionalized. Others may be living at home (their own with caregivers, or perhaps their children's). Their social opportunities may be severely restricted or harshly judged but that doesn't mean they cease to be sexual human beings.

Children of senior citizens often feel uncomfortable thinking of their parents as being sexual, just as parents may feel uncomfortable with their children's sexuality. Sometimes it takes a special effort to get beyond our family roles to see each other as having sexual feelings at all ages.

There are certain medical conditions associated with aging that may contribute to apparent sexual handicaps. It is not in the scope of this manual to consider details of these specific conditions. But it *is* in the scope of this book to remind each and every one of us that we most easily disable ourselves by believing our own illusions of disability. We can be free of these illusions by discovering and uncovering our own abilities.

CLOSING COMMENTS

This Guide provides an opportunity to focus on the elements that contribute to a balanced and whole life. The core of the Guide is self-esteem, the foundation that enables us to move securely from the self-centered existence of infancy towards relating to others. Rather than remaining a child or a frightened victim, we develop the skills needed to become members of society. We learn how to develop successful social relationships, we learn about appropriate (and inappropriate) sexual activity and hopefully we gain the ability for mature shared intimacy and happiness. Along the way as we learn about feelings and how to handle our lessons in life we role-model ourself as the person we wish to become. Thus we lead our students or clients to become more independent adults.

As professionals we study the specific needs, maturity levels, social understanding, intellectual levels, physical conditions and emotions of our students/clients. Working in a community environment we must enlist the support of parents, clergy, medical professionals, administrators and social service providers.

The most challenging parts of this Guide deal with sensitive issues of sexuality. As you tailor the activities in this Guide to best meet your students'/clients' needs and use the methods shown to gain the support needed for success, you are also giving yourself the opportunity to apply its insights, techniques and wisdom into your own life. Trust your own judgement and listen to your courageous heart!

APPENDIX A

FOUR MODEL INDIVIDUAL EDUCATIONAL PLANS (IEPS):

Individual Educational Plan: for client Jan

1. List this individual's most noticeable characteristics that indicate low self-esteem.
   a. Jan needs more social contact.
   b. Jan needs to improve her communication skills and eye contact.
   c. Jan needs to include herself in activities.
   d. Jan needs to improve her grooming, dressing, posture and body image.
   e. Jan needs to improve her confidence moving her body.
2. What are this person's strong points?
   a. Jan is open to new tasks and will take risks.
   b. Jan is an independent good worker.
   c. Jan has a friendly attitude.
3. What might be done to give recognition to these strengths?
   a. Ask Jan her opinion about things.
   b. Compliment Jan's work in one to one conversations; draw her out.
   c. Ask Jan to co-lead group activities.
   d. Give Jan a raise.
   e. Give Jan some material to sew for her own use.
   f. Encourage Jan to teach a co-worker a task.
   g. Praise Jan publicly while she's present.
   h. Use video feedback focusing on Jan's good posture, grooming and dancing.
4. Steps that staff members will take to help client to feel good about herself:
   A. Staff Member: _Don Smith_ will
      (1. Choose Jan to co-lead in group activities.
      (2. Encourage Jan to teach co-workers tasks she has learned.
      (3. Praise Jan publicly.
      (4. Ask Jan her opinion about things.
   B. Staff member: _Chris Johnson_ will
      (1. Ask Jan to co-lead activities.
      (2. Compliment Jan's work in one to one conversations; draw her out.
      (3. Spend more time talking to Jan and encouraging eye contact.
      (4. Encourage Jan to lead socialization skill group (at activities she does well).
      (5. Encourage Jan to teach other workers how to use and fix the sewing machine.
      (6. Take Jan out to lunch as a reward for looking good.
   C. Staff member: _Anne Crow_ will
      (1. Give Jan a "Hats Off" award at workshop meeting.
      (2. Make sure to greet Jan each day and ask her what she is working on.
      (3. Check with supervisor on her work assignments and help reinforce her efforts.
      (4. Ask Jan to share or demonstrate a talent she has (like lei making) and video tape at workshop meeting. Later, play back the tape with her.
   D. Staff member: _Evita Solar_ will
      (1. Pass on positive comments about Jan to and from her family.
      (2. Express pride in Jan's work to the staff, to workers and directly to Jan.
      (3. Regularly initiate social conversations with Jan reinforcing eye contact and checking for her listening comprehension.
      (4. Ask Jan to try out new ideas and materials that she can succeed at.
   E. Staff member: _Shelly White_ will
      (1. Invite Jan to join group-home people on (swimming) outing.
      (2. Present Jan with a grooming aid (mirror, hair-band, etc.).
      (3. Present Jan with an award for good work (sewing gift).

    (4. Assign Jan the role of teaching Claudette Black how to use the sewing machine.
 F. Staff member: <u>Rob Thomson</u> will
   (1. Ask Jan her opinion about work related subjects.
   (2. Compliment Jan in one to one conversations; draw her out.
   (3. Ask Jan to co-lead group exercise at client meetings.
   (4. Video Jan leading group exercise and later watch tape together praising good posture and neat appearance.
 G. Staff member: <u>Gloria Green</u> will
   (1. Give Jan a personal project to sew.
   (2. Video Jan as example of good posture, attractive grooming appearance, etc.
   (3. Praise Jan's good work in Newsletter.
   (4. Ask Jan her opinion about things during break and lunch time.

Individual Educational Plan: <u>for client Joseph</u>

1. List this individual's most noticeable characteristics that indicate low self-esteem.
 a. Joseph needs to improve his posture and body image.
 b. Joseph needs to gain flexibility in dealing with new tasks and experience.
 c. Joseph needs more socialization activities and eye contact with others.
 d. Joseph needs more options in dealing with his emotions.
2. What are this person's strong points?
 a. Joseph is helpful and outgoing with visitors.
 b. Joseph is punctual, consistent, with good attendance at work.
 c. Joseph has a good long-term memory for tasks learned and dates.
 d. Joseph has good grooming skills.
 e. Joseph enjoys working at workshop.
 f. Joseph is workshop's "town crier."
3. What might be done to give recognition to these strengths?
 a. Appoint Joseph as workshop's official "town crier" or guest greeter.
 b. Regularly practice conversations with Joseph, holding eye contact and checking for listening skills.
 c. Give Joseph more responsibilities where he can succeed on the job.
 d. Video Joseph and playback focusing on body language, "what would look better?"
 e. Praise Joseph's good posture and relaxed behavior.
4. Steps that staff members will take to help client to feel good about himself:
 A. Staff member: <u>Don Smith</u> will
   (1. Pass on positive comments to family.
   (2. Praise Joseph's good posture and relaxed behavior.
   (3. Assign Joseph to conduct orientation tours with visitors.
   (4. Acknowledge Joseph with a "Hats Off" award.
 B. Staff member: <u>Chris Johnson</u> will
   (1. Appoint Joseph as workshop's official "Town Crier" or "Guest Greeter".
   (2. Give Joseph more responsibility on the job that he can succeed at.
 C. Staff member: <u>Anne Crow</u> will
   (1. Give Joseph recognition in workshop newsletter for teaching a co-worker a task.
   (2. Regularly initiate conversation with Joseph holding eye contact and checking for listening comprehension.
   (3. Ask Joseph to report on upcoming events/dates/holidays at each workshop meeting.
   (4. Let Joseph know what I specifically appreciate about him.
 D. Staff member: <u>Evita Solar</u> will
   (1. Ask Joseph to take on special responsibilities.
   (2. Ask Joseph to share or demonstrate techniques on the job.
   (3. Praise Joseph's good work to others while he's present.
   (4. Write a "Guess Who?" sentence on board recognizing Joseph's contributions.

E. Staff member: *Marion Ferguson* will
   - (1. Regularly initiate conversations with Joseph holding eye contact and checking for listening comprehension.
   - (2. Write a letter of commendation to Joseph and give him the choice of sharing it or not sharing it with his family.
   - (3. Praise Joseph when he has good, relaxed posture.
   - (4. Give Joseph more of a variety of tasks that he can handle.
F. Staff member: *Shelly White* will
   - (1. Ask Joseph to help supervise on Wednesday mornings when she has to leave the group-home fifteen minutes early.
   - (2. Invite Joseph to join the group-home people on an outing.
   - (3. Initiate a contest to improve posture: walk with book on his head and teach others on Wednesday mornings.
   - (4. Give Joseph opportunity to report news, holidays, etc.
G. Staff member: *Rob Thomson* will
   - (1. Reinforce Joseph's good judgment or abilities such as completing tasks.
   - (2. Regularly sit down with Joseph holding eye contact and checking for listening comprehension.
   - (3. Give Joseph more of a variety of tasks to complete that he can handle.
   - (4. Encourage Joseph's good posture and relaxed behavior.
H. Staff member: *Gloria Green* will
   - (1. Video Joseph, then play back praising his good posture and relaxed behavior.
   - (2. Write letter of commendation to Joseph (he has the choice to show his Dad).
   - (3. Acknowledge Joseph's excellent attendance in workshop newsletter.
   - (4. Initiate relaxed social conversation regularly with Joseph.

Individual Educational Plan: for client Jonathan

1. List this individual's most noticeable characteristics that indicate low self-esteem.
    a. Jonathan needs more risk-taking for professional placement.
    b. Jonathan needs to be prepared for a higher functioning job outside workshop.
    c. Jonathan needs own social friends and activities.
2. What are this person's strong points?
    a. Jonathan is outgoing verbally with visitors.
    b. Jonathan has leadership skills.
    c. Jonathan plays guitar and sings.
    d. Jonathan is an independent, consistent, polite, punctual worker.
    e. Jonathan has a good sense of humor.
    f. Jonathan is informed on current events.
3. What might be done to give recognition to these strengths?
    a. Assign co-leadership or organizer roles to Jonathan at workshop functions.
    b. Include Jonathan in staff social functions.
    c. Be Jonathan's co-facilitator with group discussions.
    d. Give Jonathan the responsibility of reporting current events at workshop.
    e. Encourage Jonathan to join the YMCA/Association for the Blind/Guitar Club, etc.
4. Steps that staff members will take to help client to feel good about himself:
    A. Staff member: *Don Smith* will
       - (1. Ask Jonathan for input on decisions on the job.
       - (2. Ask Jonathan to take on special responsibilities.
       - (3. Try out new ideas and materials with Jonathan.
       - (4. Express confidence in his ability to succeed.
    B. Staff member: *Chris Johnson* will
       - (1. Include Jonathan in staff social functions.
       - (2. Be a co-facilitator with Jonathan at workshop meetings.
    C. Staff member: *Anne Crow* will
       - (1. Acknowledge Jonathan's reliability in the newsletter.

(2. Ask him to dictate a newsletter article.
(3. Co-facilitate group discussions with Jonathan.
(4. Acknowledge Jonathan for coordinating responsibilities with a "Hats Off" award.
   D. Staff member: <u>Evita Solar</u> will
(1. Pass on positive comments to and from Jonathan's family.
(2. Take Jonathan out to lunch.
(3. Share with Jonathan outstanding things observed and appreciated.
(4. Express confidence in Jonathan's ability to succeed.
   E. Staff member: <u>Marion Ferguson</u> will
(1. Involve Jonathan in leadership roles (ex: play guitar, emcee events, etc.).
(2. Encourage Jonathan to join social groups.
(3. Encourage Jonathan to make his own decisions.
(4. Encourage lunch time guitar playing for others.
   F. Staff member: <u>Shelly White</u> will
(1. Invite Jonathan to group parties.
(2. Ask Jonathan to help others hear; to be someone's ears.

Individual Educational Plan: <u>for client Claudette</u>

1. List this individual's most noticeable characteristics that indicate low self-esteem.
   a. Claudette needs to learn appropriate behavior in public.
   b. Claudette needs to learn to make eye contact.
   c. Claudette needs to recognize and deal appropriately with her emotions.
   d. Claudette needs to improve her self-image.
2. What are this person's strong points?
   a. Claudette likes to read and write her thoughts.
   b. Claudette likes children.
   c. Claudette is punctual and helpful at work.
   d. Claudette is a good listener.
   e. Claudette has a good sense of humor.
   f. Claudette has housecleaning and self-care skills.
3. What might be done to give recognition to these strengths?
   a. Strongly encourage Claudette to write a story, article or column in each workshop newsletter.
   b. Teach Claudette to style her hair and make-up attractively.
   c. Encourage Claudette to attend a weight reduction program.
   d. After Claudette learns to style her own hair and make-up, encourage her to teach someone else how to take care of their hair and make-up.
   e. Compliment Claudette publicly for positive behaviors and be specific.
   f. Encourage Claudette to read her writing at workshop meetings.
   g. Encourage Claudette in leadership roles with co-workers.
4. Steps that staff members will take to help client to feel good about himself:
   A. Staff member: <u>John Carroll</u> will
(1. Ask Claudette to take on special responsibilities.
(2. Express confidence in Claudette's ability to succeed.
(3. Compliment Claudette publicly for positive behavior.
(4. Encourage Claudette to read her writing at workshop meetings.
   B. Staff member: <u>Chris Johnson</u> will
(1. Encourage Claudette in leadership roles with lower functioning workers.
   C. Staff member: <u>Anne Crow</u> will
(1. Strongly encourage Claudette to write a column (Ex: "Claudette's Commentaries") in the newsletter.
(2. Compliment Claudette's positive behaviors.
(3. Make an effort to talk to Claudette before work begins.
(4. Reward Claudette with a "Hats Off" award.

D. Staff member: *Evita Solar* will
- *(1. Express confidence in Claudette's ability to succeed.*
- *(2. Attach a balloon to Claudette's chair when she is behaving appropriately.*
- *(3. Write Claudette a personal letter of recognition and thanks.*
- *(4. Encourage Claudette to write a news article.*

E. Staff member: *Marion Ferguson* will
- *(1. Give Claudette more responsibility as supervisor and helper.*
- *(2. Ask Claudette for suggestions, advice and input on problems.*
- *(3. Compliment Claudette for positive behaviors.*
- *(4. Encourage Claudette to bake a cake for birthdays at workshop.*

APPENDIX B

HELPING PARENTS DEAL WITH THE SEXUALITY OF THEIR SON OR DAUGHTER WITH SPECIAL NEEDS
Winifred Kempton, M.S.S.

This outline asks nine questions of your students' or group's parents and then offers answers and solutions. It is reprinted here to provide further activities for your parents' support group.

Being involved with students who are slow learners usually means being involved with their parents and unless the son or daughter is institutionalized permanently, much of the success of what is done for them by someone outside the family depends on their parents' cooperation and understanding. Some parents will reinforce; some will interfere.

There are many complaints from teachers, social workers and others working with challenged individuals that parental attitudes concerning their son's or daughter's sexuality cause complications that impair their constructive efforts. Consequently, how parents feel about their own, as well as their child's sexuality, must be of concern and that constant efforts must be made to reach them. Therefore, knowledge and skills in understanding and helping the parents is vitally important in this training course.

Helping parents is not a simple matter. There are many special complications because of the highly diversified needs of parents depending upon the age of the son or daughter, the level of intelligence, social functioning and the living situation (institutional, foster home, own home, etc.). There <u>are</u> some basic facts, however, which are important for the professional to keep in mind in working with all parents. These facts can be presented to the course participants with the following questions and answers outline form:

Question 1
What is the word that best describes the feelings of every parent in relation to their children's sexuality?
  Answer:
- Anxiety.

Question 2
What characteristics do most parents share in relation to human sexuality?
  Answers:
- Uncomfortable and embarrassed when discussing it.
- Ignorant of many facts concerning reproductive process.
- Misguided by myths and misinformation.
- Confused about morality and values.
- Harbor guilt feelings about their own sexual thoughts and behavior.

Question 3
What are special concerns of the parents of slow learners?
  Answers:
- That their children will not be able to control their sexual impulses so that they:
    Will embarrass them socially.
    Will get into trouble with the law.
    Will bear children which will add a burden to them.
- That others will exploit them sexually.

- That if they don't have the traditional outlet for sexual impulses (sexual intercourse) it will affect their minds, be unhealthy for them or cause them to commit violent acts.

Question 4
Why is it especially difficult to help parents with their son's or daughter's sexuality?
Answers:
- Their attitudes towards sexuality vary so widely, according to their own early conditioning.
- Many have tended to ignore the sexuality of their children and are bewildered by a change in thinking.
- Their children vary so widely intellectually, emotionally and in ability to function that help must be highly individualized.
- They have few models to follow and few experts to guide them.

Question 5
What are some important goals in working with parents?
Answers:
- Relieve their anxieties whatever they may be.
- Help them to accept their son or daughter as a sexual being.
- Help them to see the sexual nature of their son or daughter as being an integral part of his or her total personality.
- That their son or daughter needs help in understanding sexuality more than others.
- To help set realistic goals for their son's or daughter's sexual behavior and sexual fulfillment.
- Offer them direct information and support.
- Help them understand masturbation and how they should deal with it.

Question 6
What reasons would be given parents as to why children who are slow learners need sex education more than other children?
Answers:
- They usually over respond to attention and give affection indiscriminantly in return.
- They often have poor judgment and deficient ability to use reason in developing and carrying on relationships.
- They often cannot explain or verbalize their feelings, thoughts or experiences.
- Because so many do not reach emotional maturity, they are generally inept in delaying gratification whether it be an ice cream cone or sexual intercourse
- They often do whatever is asked of them without questioning and consequently are more likely to be exploited.
- They do not have same access to accurate information from peers.
- They often do not have a ready ability to distinguish reality from unreality and believe myths and half truths more readily.

Question 7
What do parents need to understand in regard to sex education?
Answers:
- Sex education begins at birth. Attitudes are developed and sensual pleasures are learned from infancy from many varied sources.

- Sex education goes on at all times, in most places from many different media. The question is, not <u>if</u> their child should have sex education but <u>how</u> and by <u>whom</u>.
- Sex education includes learning about:
    Relationships.
    Body sensations, their stimulation and control.
    Human reproductive physiology including male and female roles.
- Sex education does not breed experimentation nor stimulate or motivate the student to sexual activity. Rather, it acts as a deterrent, for it teaches responsibility and control.
- Sex education cannot be premature - a child will learn only what she or he is capable of comprehending. It can be too late - for example, preparing a girl for menstruation must be done prior to her menarche.
- Sex education will enrich their child's life and give her or him added self-esteem.

Question 8
What are other facts about sexuality that parents should know?
Answers:
- Sexuality is an integral part of the total personality and it cannot be separate. Good sexual adjustment usually occurs in a well adjusted person.
- Humans are born with sexual drives but not goals. Sexual intercourse is not the only satisfactory form of sexual expression.
- To admit arousal usually means the capacity to control sexual impulses.
- Sexual thoughts are normal and do not harm as long as they do not hurt others and are not directed towards inappropriate irresponsible behavior.

Question 9
What are some other aspects that should be presented and discussed with parents in relation to the sexuality of their sons or daughters?
Answers:
- When the child is growing up it is unwise to create the impression that having babies is important and that mating is necessary in order to be considered normal or fulfilled in our society.
- Do not overprotect their daughter out of fear of pregnancy to the extent that her pleasures are sacrificed. Nor should the parents rely solely on the daughter's judgment to cope with sexual situations (an answer can be to take proper precautions through birth control).
- Continue to attempt to keep an open relationship so that the child (or adult) will report activities, especially in situations where they may be manipulated, coerced or involved in sexual activity that may cause them problems.
- We advise parents to not give their special needs child more affection or have them return it more than the other children in family. It can be confusing or stimulating and can channel them into promiscuous habits or get them into trouble later on with strangers.
- Giving their child a sense of self-worth may protect him or her from seeking approval or recognition through inappropriate sexual activity later on.
- Masturbation is done in private and in a non-compulsive self-punishing manner. It is a normal, safe way for sexual expression/gratification.
- Encourage parents to provide their sons and daughters with opportunities for enjoyable social relationships.

At all times it should be emphasized that parents must be helped to be more comfortable about their own and their son's or daughter's sexuality - that it is natural that they will have difficulty because they had no model to follow - but that it can be overcome by courage and persistence.

RESOURCES

REFERENCES

Blum, G., and Blum, B., *Feeling Good Playful Question Cards and instruction booklet.* Feeling Good Associates, 77-6502 Marlin Road, Kailua-Kona, Hawaii 96740, (808) 326-4192, e-mail: goliard@aloha.net. (A non-competitive, non-threatening game containing 80 fun, thought-energizing question cards which can be played with adults, seniors, families, children and in school (regular and special education). Excellent for breaking the ice and stimulating discussions. With no wrong answers, the game can be played with multiple variations.)

Calderwood, Deryck,. *About Your Sexuality.* Boston: Unitarian Universalist Associates. This book is out of print. Check www.BookFinder.com for availability. ISBN: 0-933840-60-8 / 0933840608.

De la Cruz, F., LaVeck, G.D. (editors) 1973. *Human Sexuality and the Mentally Retarded.* New York, Brunner/Mazel.

Dodson, B. 1974. *Sex for One: The Joy of Selfloving.* New York: Betty Dodson, P.O. Box 1933, New York 10156, (866) 877-9676, www.bettydodson.com (A cross between a personal narrative about the pitfalls of romantic love versus erotic sex and an impassioned defense of masturbation.)

Golas, T. 2002. *The Lazy Man's Guide to Enlightenment.* Palo Alto, California: Gibbs Smith Publishers.

Gunther, B. 1986. *Sense Relaxation.* New York: MacMillan.

Heslinga, K., Schellen, A., and Verkuyl, A. 1974. *Not Made of Stone: The Sexual Problems of Handicapped People.* Springfield, IL: Charles C. Thomas. Out of print.

Katchadourian, H. and Lunde, D. 1972. *Fundamentals of Human Sexuality.* New York: Holt, Rinehart, and Winston. Out of print.

Laskow, L., 1992. *Healing With Love.* San Francisco: Harper.

Malamud, D., and Machover, S. 1975. *Toward Self Understanding.* Springfield, Illinois: Charles C. Thomas. Out of print.

Reproductive Anatomy Charts. Planned Parenthood of Minnesota, 1965 Ford Parkway, St. Paul, MN 55116, (612) 698-2401. (Male and female body charts, life-size on heavy paper with detachable parts to demonstrate erection, ejaculation, urination, menstruation, pelvic examinations, fertility, and fetal development.)

Reproductive Anatomy Models. Jim Jackson and Co., 30 Buena Vista Park, Cambridge, MA 02140, (617) 864-9063, (800) 827-9063. (Three-dimensional cross-sectional models of the female and male reproductive systems, including flaccid and erect penis models. Instructor guides to reproductive anatomy models and catalog of anatomic models are available.)

Schwartz, L. 1981. *The World of the Unborn: Nurturing Your Child Before Birth.* New York: Marek.

Spitz and Bowlby, 1971. *Rock-a-Bye-Baby,* A Time-Life Documentary Film (28 min). Available from McGraw-Hill; executive producer: Lothar Wolff. (Demonstrates the concept of critical period and the behavior of mother-deprived institutionalized children.) It may also be downloaded from the Internet: www.humanist.de/fpx/rockabyebaby-small.rm; or www.humanist.de/fpx/rockabyebaby-big.rm

Virtue, D. 1999. *Healing With The Angels - Oracle Cards,* Hay House Inc., P.O. Box 5100, Carlsbad, CA 92018, www.hayhouse.com. (Guidebook and cards – helpful tool for coping and seeing the positive side of life's lessons.)

SELF-ESTEEM

Bailey, S. D., 1994 *Wings to Fly: Bringing Theatre Arts to Students with Special Needs,* Blue Tower Training Center (866) 258-8266. (A comprehensive nuts and bolts handbook which describes concrete, proven techniques and lesson plans to make drama accessible to people with disabilities. Useful in prevention education skits and productions performed by people with developmental disabilities.)

Battle, J. 1981. *Culture-Free Self-Esteem Inventories for Children and Adults.* Austin, Texas: Pro Ed Publishing Co. wwwww.proedinc.com, (800) 897-3202.

Edwards, J. 1980. *Being Me: A Socio-Sexual Training Guide.* Portland, OR: Edneck Communications. Out of print.

Ludwig, S., *Sexuality, A Curriculum for Individuals Who Have Difficulty With Traditional Learning Methods.* (905) 940-1333. (An excellent book with a curriculum on a variety of topics including feelings, self-esteem and assertiveness. Includes a variety of activities for persons of various functioning levels. Easy to use). See also the Sexual Health Network: www.SexualHealth.com

SEX INFORMATION AND SEX EDUCATION – GENERAL

Goldstone, S, 1999. *The Ins and Outs of Gay Sex,* A Medical Handbook for Men, Dell trade paperback.

Gordon, S., *All Families Are Different* (ages 8-12). Amherst, NY: Prometheus Books, www.prometheusbooks.com, (800) 421-0351.

Gordon, S. 1992. *A Better Safe Than Sorry Book.* (ages 5-9) Amherst, NY: Prometheus Books, www.prometheusbooks.com, (800) 421-0351.

Gordon, S. 1974. *Did the Sun Shine Before You Were Born?* Amherst, NY: Prometheus Books, www.prometheusbooks.com, (800) 421-0351.

Gordon, S. 1992. *Facts About Sex for Today's Youth.* (ages 9-14) Amherst, NY: Prometheus Books, www.prometheusbooks.com, (800) 421-0351.

Gordon, S., *Girls Are Girls, and Boys Are Boys – So What's the Difference?* (ages 6-9). Amherst, NY: Prometheus Books, www.prometheusbooks.com, (800) 421-0351.

Gordon, S. 2000. *How Can You Tell If You're Really In Love?* Avon, MA: Adams Media.

Gordon, S. 2000. *Raising A Child Conservatively.* Avon, MA: Adams Media.

Nilsson, L., Ingelman-Sundberg, A., Wirsen, C., 1986. *A Child Is Born.* New York: Dell.

Sarrell, L., and Sarrell, P., 1979. *Sexual Unfolding.* Boston : Little, Brown.

Waxman, S. 1989. *What Is A Girl? What Is A Boy?* Culver City, CA: Ty Crowell Co.

SEX INFORMATION AND SEX EDUCATION
– FOR PEOPLE WHO ARE PHYSICALLY HANDICAPPED

Doughten, S. D., et al. 1978. *Signs for Sexuality: A Resource Manual for Teaching Sexuality to the Deaf.* Seattle: Planned Parenthood.

Robinault, I. 1978. *Sex, Society and the Disabled.* Hagerstown, Maryland: Harper and Row. Out of print.

Task Force on Concerns of Physically Disabled Women. 1978. *Toward Intimacy: Family Planning and Sexuality Concerns of Physically Disabled Women.* Also: *Within Reach: Providing Family Planning Service to Physically Disabled Women.* New York: Human Sciences Press.

Widening The Circle: Sexual Assault and People with Disabilities and the Elderly, Manual And Resource Guide. Wisconsin Coalition Against Sexual Assault, Inc. (608) 257-1516. Website: www.wcasa.org. (Structured to assist sexual assault service providers, human service personnel and others to widen the circle of our communities to include all of us who are vulnerable to being victims/survivors of sexual violence.)

SEX INFORMATION AND SEX EDUCATION
– FOR PEOPLE WHO ARE SLOW LEARNERS

All of Us Talking Together, Video and Instructional Guideline. Program Development Associates, 800-452-0710. (Designed to address the need for sex education of persons with developmental disabilities. Includes a sex education segment of reproductive anatomy, pregnancy, contraception and disease prevention.)

Anderson, O.H., 2000. *Doing What Comes Naturally: Dispelling Myths and Fallacies About Sexuality and People with Developmental Disabilities.* High Tide Press, 3650 W. 183rd St., Homewood, IL 60430.

Brown, G., Carney, P., Cortis, J., Metz, L., Petrie, A*., Human Sexuality Handbook: Guiding People Toward Positive Expressions of Sexuality.* The Association for Community Living, Residential Services, One Carando Drive, Springfield, MA. 01104-3211.

The Exceptional Parent. Pay-Ed Corporation, 96 Bokleston Street, Boston, MA 02116. (Monthly magazine with practical information about children with disabilities.)

Heaton, C., 1995. *Let's Talk About Health.* The ARC of New Jersey. North Brunswick, NJ. (This book was designed for women with developmental disabilities. It covers a variety of topics related to women's health issues and being a woman.) Out of print.

Hingsburger, D., *I OPENERS: Parents Ask Questions About Sexuality and Children with Developmental Disabilities.* Mariah Management (800) 856-5007. (The author answers real questions about sexuality from parents of children with developmental disabilities. He provides practical answers in a straightforward, sensitive, sometimes humorous, and honest manner.)

Hingsburger, D. *Just Say Know.* Diverse City Press, 13561 Leslie St., Richmond Hill, Ontario, L4E 1A2, Canada.

Hingsburger, D., and Harper, M., *The Ethics of Touch: Establishing and Maintaining Appropriate Boundaries in Service to People with Developmental Disabilities.* A video. Diverse City Press, 13561 Leslie St., Richmond Hill, Ontario, L4E 1A2, Canada. (The author answers difficult questions about touch, privacy and boundaries. He provides many practical solutions to problems related to teaching healthy sexuality to persons with developmental disabilities. A manual is included to guide service providers through the learning process.)

Kempton, W. and McKee, L. 2002. *An Easy Guide to Loving Carefully for Men and Women.* Winifred Kempton Associates, 3300 Darby Road C-404, Haverford, PA. 19041.

Kempton, W., and Forman, R. 1976. *Guidelines on Training In Sexuality and the Mentally Handicapped.* Winifred Kempton Associates, 3300 Darby Road C-404, Haverford, PA. 19041.

Kempton, W., et al. 1979. *Love, Sex and Birth Control for the Mentally Retarded, Guide for Parents.* Winifred Kempton Associates, 3300 Darby Road C-404, Haverford, PA. 19041.

Kempton, W., *Socialization and Sexuality.* Winifred Kempton Associates, 3300 Darby Road C-404, Haverford, PA. 19041. (A comprehensive training guide that teaches service providers and parents how to teach people with disabilities about social and sexual issues. Includes sexuality education and guidelines for curriculum design, coping with inappropriate sexual behavior, informed consent, sexual abuse and much more.)

Perske, R. 1973. *New Directions: For Parents of Persons Who Are Retarded.* Nashville: Abingdon Press.

Person to Person, Video and Discussion Guide. CHOICES, Inc. (202) 364-5303. (Open communication about sexuality with parents, service providers and persons with developmental disabilities. Demonstrates parents discussing sexuality issues in a frank and sensitive manner.)

Roots & Wings, Video on Sexuality Education. CHOICES, Inc. (202) 364-5303. (For teenagers with cognitive disabilities. In this video you meet several teens with special needs and watch parents and caregivers prepare them for adulthood.)

Schwier, K. M., and Hingsburger, D., *Sexuality: Your Sons and Daughters with Intellectual Disabilities.* Paul H. Brookes Publishing Company.

SIECUS Publications 2003. *A Bibliography of Resources In Sex Education for the Mentally Retarded.* New York: Human Sciences Press.

ABUSE PREVENTION BOOKS, GUIDES, TOOLS

Aunt Rita's Patient. Illustrated teacher's guide and student workbook/storybook for ages 4-6. American Red Cross-Lakeland Chapter, 2131 Deckner Ave., P.O. Box 8295, Green Bay, WI 54308 (Describing the life of a person with AIDS.)

Anderson, O.H., Paceley, S., *Safe Beginnings: Protecting Our Children from Sexual Abuse.* Blue Tower Training Center, (866) 258-8266. (Comprehensive sexual abuse prevention book for parents, professionals, child care providers and others who care about preschool children. Includes facts about sexual abuse; issues that need healing in our personal histories; how to teach prevention skills to young children; teaching skills to children with disabilities; how to create safer child care settings; how to identify potential sex offenders; how to create a safer world through social change; and much more.)

Anderson, O.H., Paceley, S., *Genesis: In the Beginning...Breaking the Cycle of Sexual Abuse.* Blue Tower Training Center. (866) 258-8266. (Instructional guide for parents of children with developmental disabilities.)

Baladerian, N. J., *Abuse of Children and Adults with Disabilities: A Risk Reduction and Intervention Guide for Parents and Other Advocates.* Disability and Personal Rights Project (310) 281-6131. E-mail: DrNora@doctor.com.

Baladerian, N. J., *Interviewing Skills To Use With Abuse Victims Who Have Developmental Disabilities.* Mental Health Consultants, c/o Nora Baladerian, P.O. Box T, Culver City, CA 90230.

Fink, M., C.S.W., *Reducing Vulnerability.* Learning Publications (800) 222-1525. E-mail: info@learingpublications.com. (Curriculum is organized in three units: 1-Child Sexual Abuse Prevention; 2-Teasing, Bullying and Sexual Harassment Prevention; 3-Child Abduction Prevention. Each unit contains notes to presenters, teaching guidelines, resource and curriculum materials.)

Heighway, S., and Webster, S.K., *Skills Training for Assertiveness, Relationship-Building and Sexual Awareness (STARS).* Susan Heighway, P.O. Box 5122, Madison, WI 53705, (608) 263-5996. (Designed to teach people with disabilities ways to find appropriate sexual expression that fit their developmental needs. Includes skills training to engage in beneficial friendships, boundaries and respect.)

Keeping Yourself Safe...At Home...At Work...And in the Community. Network of Victim Assistance (NOVA) (215) 348-5664. (The focus of this curriculum is self-empowerment through knowledge and the practice of personal safety skills at home, work and in the community.)

Kempton, W., McKee, L., Stiggall-Muccigrosso, L., illustrated by V. Cohen, *An Easy Guide to Loving Carefully.* Winifred Kempton Associates, 3300 Darby Road C-404, Haverford, PA. 19041. (Book about the sexual parts of women's and men's bodies, sexual health and sexual feelings. It also tells how to prevent unplanned pregnancies and about sexually transmitted diseases.)

Laesch, S. and Paceley, S., 2004. *WE CAN Stop Abuse: A Sexual Abuse Prevention Curriculum for persons with developmental disabilities.* Blue Tower Training Center. www.maconresources.org.

Mansell, S., and Sobsey, D., 2001. *Counseling People with Developmental Disabilities Who Have Been Sexually Abused.* National Association for Persons with Developmental Disabilities and Mental Health Needs (NADD), 132 Fair Street, Kingston, New York 12401.

Paceley, S., illustrated by Penhallegon, A.R., 2001. *My Body...My Choice.* Blue Tower Training Center (866) 258-8266, www.maconresources.org. (Illustrated book on sexual abuse prevention written for adolescents and adults with developmental disabilities.)

Paceley, S. and Laesch, S., 2003 *WE CAN Stop Abuse, Peer Training Manual.* Blue Tower Training Center (866) 258-8266. (How to empower people with developmental disabilities to teach their peers to resist and report sexual abuse. Includes a curriculum as well as activities that can be utilized by peer trainers to teach others.)

Pease, T., Ph.D. and Franz, B., MS., *Your Safety, Your Rights. Personal Safety and Abuse Prevention Education Program to Empower Adults with Disabilities and Train Service Providers.* Network of Victim Assistance (NOVA), Pennsylvania Coalition Against Rape (215) 348-5664. (A manual that includes a curriculum for adults with developmental disabilities as well as information for instructors. Topics include individual rights, myths, personal safety, healthy relationships, indicators of sexual assault, how to handle disclosures and more.)

Personal Space...Safety Planning Awareness Choice Empowerment: A Violence Prevention Program for Women. Available at no cost from the ARC of Maryland. Website: www.thearcmd.org. (Manual includes a complete training program for women with developmental disabilities to empower them to prevent violence. It includes detailed information to develop classes and lesson plans plus other information.)

Plummer, C., *Preventing Sexual Abuse - Activities and Strategies for Those Working with Children and Adolescents.* Learning Publications, (800) 222-1525. E-mail: info@learningpublications.com. (Curriculum guide for K-12 and persons with developmental disabilities.)

Sexuality Safety Skills and Support Needs Assessment Tool. Ray Graham Association, 2801 Finley Road, Downers Grove, Il. 60515. (This tool identifies skills, interests and support needs related to safety and capacity to consent.)

Voelker, E. and Wolfe, M., *Professional Guide for Identifying Sexual Assault in Individuals With Developmental Disabilities.* Victim Outreach Intervention Center and Pennsylvania Coalition Against Rape (PCAR), www.pcar.org. (Covers the basics of identifying sexual abuse in persons with developmental disabilities. Includes a PowerPoint presentation.)

Victim Outreach Intervention Center., *Sexual Assault Prevention for Individuals With Developmental Disabilities.* Pennsylvania Coalition Against Rape, (800) 692-7445, www.pcar.org. (Curriculum includes a teaching guide and video.)

Winkler, Henry, 1989. *Strong Kids, Safe Kids.* Video: Paramount Studio. (Children are taught how to protect themselves from sexual abuse.)

GAMES

Touch Study Cards. Illusion Theatre, Minneapolis, MN 55403. (Contains thirteen study cards with each set; meant to provide a simple, clear visual aid and discussion tool for educators and counselors.)

AUDIO-VISUAL MATERIALS - CHARTS, VIDEOS, DVDs, FILMSTRIPS, FILMS, SLIDE KITS
A Day in the Life of Bonnie Consolo. A great film about a very able woman born without arms. Barr Films, 100 Wilshire Blvd., Santa Monica, California 90401

Bartlett, V. and Brock, N., *Looking for Me.* Classic film provides a unique record of dance therapist Janet Adler working to develop movement awareness with normal and emotionally disturbed children. The highlight is an unforgettable sequence showing two autistic girls being brought out of their shells. University of California Extension, Center for Media and Independent Learning, 1995 University Avenue, Berkeley, CA 94704. (Catalog #37131)

Blum, G. and Blum, B., *"I Can Say No!"* Sound filmstrip transferred onto DVD. Includes teacher's guide. Students (disabled and nondisabled) learn how to say "no" without mixed messages and with confidence even under peer pressure. Three trigger situations are introduced using teen actors and actresses saying "no" to shoplifting; saying "no" to a bully; and saying "no" to smoking marijuana. The program is success-oriented, fostering self-esteem and preventing sexual abuse in society. Feeling Good Associates, 77-6502 Marlin Rd. Kailua-Kona, HI 96740.

Kempton, W., *Life Horizons.* Nine different slide presentations to teach persons with mental retardation the basic aspects of sexuality and related behavior. Includes teacher's guide. Covers the following topics: Parts of the Body including masturbation and nocturnal emissions, Female Puberty, Social Behavior, Human Reproduction, Fertility Regulation, STD, Marriage and Parenting. Stanfield House, P.O. Box 41058, Santa Barbara, CA 93140.

Netter, F. H., *Atlas of Human Anatomy,* CIBA-GEIGY Corp., West Caldwell, NJ 07006. Plates 393 and 394: Realistic drawings of corresponding parts of male and female anatomy including diagrams of the homologues of the external and internal genitalia.

OTHER RECOMMENDED READING
Brandon, N. 1985. *Honoring the Self; Self-Esteem and Personal Transformation.* Bantam Books.

Buscaglia, L. 1972. *Love.* Thorofare, New Jersey: Charles B. Slack.

Canfield, J., and Wells, H. C. 1976. *100 Ways To Self-Esteem.* Englewood Cliffs, New Jersey: Prentice Hall.

Dass, Ram. 1971. *Remember - Be Here Now.* New York: Crown.

Foundation for Inner Peace. 1975. *A Course In Miracles.* New York: Coleman Graphics.

Godek, G.J.P., 1997. *Love, The Course They Forgot to Teach You in School,* Napervile, IL: Casablanca Press/Division of Sourcebooks, Inc.

Gordon, S. 2004. *When Living Hurts*: Union for Reform Judaism Press, 633 Third Avenue - New York, NY 10017 (Best-selling book for teenagers in distress. Helps young people who feel discouraged, sad, lonely, bored or even suicidal, recognize their feelings and cope. Includes updated material on homosexuality and a new section on AIDS.)

Gordon, S. and Shimberg, E. 2004. *Another Chance for Love – Finding A Partner In Later Life,* Avon, MA, Adams Media, www.adamsmedia.com.

Gordon, S. 2000. *A Friend in Need - How to Help When Times Are Tough,* Amherst, NY: Prometheus Books, www.prometheusbooks.com, (800) 421-0351.

Jampolsky, G. 1979. *Love Is Letting Go Of Fear.* Millbrae, California: Celestial Arts.

Nickerson, C., Lollis, C., and Porter, E. 1980. *Miraculous Me.* Seattle: Comprehensive Health Education Foundation (www.amazon.com). Out of print.

Satir, V. 1975. *Self-Esteem.* Millbrae, California: Celestial Arts.

Satir, V. 1976. *Making Contact.* Millbrae, California: Celestial Arts.

Shyer, M. 1988. *Welcome Home, Jellybean.* New York: Aladdin Library.
Stevens, J. 1973. *Awareness: Exploring, Experimenting, Experiencing.* Bantam Books. Out of print.
Williamson, M. 1993. *A Woman's Worth.* New York: Ballantine Books, Random House.

RESOURCE SCIENTIFIC ORGANIZATIONS

AASECT. American Association of Sex Educators, Counselors and Therapists. One East Wacker Drive, Suite 2700, Chicago, Illinois 60601. (312) 222-1717.

SIECUS. Sex Information and Educational Council of the United States. 84 Fifth Avenue, Suite 407, New York, New York 10011. Clearinghouse for sex information and resources primarily for professionals working in the field.

SSSS. Society for the Scientific Study of Sex, P.O. Box 416, Allentown, PA 18105, www.sexscience.org.